A
MEI YA
INTERNATIONAL EDITION

CLASSICAL CHINESE PLAYS

CLASSICAL CHINESE PLAYS

Josephine Huang Hung

DRAMA BOOK SPECIALISTS/PUBLISHERS

150 West 52nd Street

New York, New York 10019

This book is in the Mei Ya Heritage Series

In Memory of My Parents

PREFACE TO THE FIRST EDITION

Although about four hundred plays are being performed on the Chinese-opera stage today, very few have been introduced to the Western world. This seems to be due to the neglect of Chinese scholars, who have translated other literary forms into foreign languages, but rarely Chinese operatic plays. Traditionally Chinese scholars have looked on drama with contempt, though most of them have a personal passion for the theater. It may also be because the bare bones of a libretto appearing in black ink on white paper convey hardly any of the esthetic beauty of this art form to the reader; the music, singing, symbolic acting, gorgeous costuming, and stagecraft are really more the essence of this art than its word-skeleton. Be that as it may, I believe even such stark stems stripped of their flowers may be helpful to a non-Chinese interested in our drama.

This book contains translations of five of the most popular plays of the Chinese opera, with an introduction and notes. I hope this may bring to the reader some understanding of the structure of the Chinese opera and thereby he may sense the fragrance of the Chinese plays. I also hope he may come to know something about the Chinese people through reading these plays which, like all drama, mirror the life and culture of China. At the same time, he may learn that the human heart and mind are about the same all over the world by discovering his own problems, passions, and aspirations reflected in the plays.

The plays selected for this volume belong to the wen-hsi, plays about social and domestic life. The five plays are: The Faithful Harlot (Yü T'ang Ch'un 玉堂春), Two Men on a String (Feng Yi T'ing:鳳儀亭), Twice a Bride (Hung Luan Hsi:鴻鸞禧), One Missing Head (Chiu Keng T'ien:九更天), *and* The Price of Wine (Mei Lung Chen:梅龍鎮). *They are of unknown authorship and date, but they have been great favorites of Chinese theater-goers for the last few hundred years. Aside from* Two Men on a String and Twice a Bride, *where I have interpolated the suggestions of some simple settings as would be found in a Western play, the translations follow the original stories as closely as the divergent idioms of the Chinese and English languages permit–except for some necessary condensations–so the plays retain the flavor of production on the Chinese stage. Unless otherwise made clear by context, all mention of "left" or "right" on the stage should be understood to be from the viewpoint of the stage. In the romanization of all the terms and names in this volume, the Wade-Giles system has been used.*

In writing this book, I am deeply indebted to Mrs. Eleanor B. Hicks for her editorial assistance; to Dr. Ch'i Ju-shan, the great authority on the Chinese opera, for his valuable information; and, most of all, to Mr. John A. Bottorff for his patient and abiding interest in the project, constant encouragement, criticism, and helpful suggestions. A word of thanks is also due Mrs. Helen Sha for the typing of my original manuscript.

Taipei, Taiwan
Nov. 20, 1961

Josephine Huang Hung

PREFACE TO THE SECOND EDITION

The first edition of this book was an attempt to introduce Chinese classical drama to the West primarily through reading. Little did I expect, though I secretly hoped, that some day the plays represented in this volume would produced on the western stage. To my delight and gratification, all the five plays had been produced abroad and with great success.

Aside from *Two Men on a String,* re-entitled *The Beautiful Bait,* which was produced in Chinese by the Foo Hsing School of Dramatic Arts, Taiwan, on their tour to the United States, Canada, Central and South Americas, the other four plays were presented in English from the adaptations and translations of this volume. *Twice a Bride* was first produced by the University of Hawaii in May, 1963 and then at Hanover College, Indiana, in March, 1967. Both productions enjoyed great success. This was the first foreign play so enthusiastically received in Honolulu that it was sent on a tour to the neighboring islands. *The Price, of Wine* was produced at Grinnell College, Iowa, under my own supervision while I was a visiting Fulbright-Hayes professor there in the fall semester of 1963. It was performed by the students of my Chinese drama class before eager and appreciative full-house audiences, both at Grinnell College and at the State University of Iowa. It was the first time that a Chinese classical play in English was presented in the middle west of the United States. *The Faithful Harlot* was first produced in Elizabeth City, South Africa, in 1964, and then by the Grand Hotel Drama Guild in Taipei, in July, 1968. *One Missing Head* was presented for the first time outside of China at the University of North Carolina at Greensboro in 1967 when I was again a Fulbright professor in the United States. It was highly praised and won many excellent reviews from the leading newspapers of Greensboro and the vicinities.

The productions of these plays abroad conveyed the spirit of Chinese classical drama and have demonstrated that the highly stylized Chinese theatre is not beyond the capabilities of Western actors, nor is it beyond the appreciation of Western audiences. With this in mind, I am encouraged to adapt more plays into English. Furthermore, in producing the plays myself, I realized the necessity of filling the skeleton of the plays with flowers and leaves so as to make them more dramatic and comprehensible to the audience and reader. Therefore in this edition, I have attempted to add some stage directions and more scenes, and some photographs of the American productions are also inserted to give life to the reading or performance.

The first edition of this book has been translated into Spanish by Josefina Martinez as *Teatro de Opera* and published by Editorial Sudamericna, Buenos Aires, Argentina, in 1963; and into French by René Bessier as *Les Enfants du Jardin Enchante* in Africa and published by Heritage Press, Taipei, in 1965. I still have the hope that Chinese culture will be introduced to the West by the production and reading of these and other Chinese plays, not only in Chinese and English, but also in Spanish, French and other languages.

Taipei, Taiwan
September, 1970

Josephine Huang Hung

CONTENTS

ILLUSTRATIONS

Four artists have contributed to this book. The cover, by **Chang Ta Hsia** (張大夏), shows Yu Nu, heroine of *Twice a Bride,* talking to the scholar-beggar Mo Chi.

Sketches of the stage, actors, musical instruments and stage props are by **Chang Ta-hsia** (張大夏).

P'i Ta-ch'un (邳大椿) contributed the four paintings showing differing types of facial make-up and **Paul Kuo** (郭博修) executed the vignettes used at the opening of each chapter.

The frontispiece, a photograph by **Chin-san Long** (郎靜山), shows Miss **Hsü Lu** (徐 露), star of Taipei's Ta P'eng Capital Opera Troupe, as she appears in the role of Tiao Ch'an dancing in her father's garden. (See *Two Men on a String*).

INTRODUCTION TO CLASSICAL CHINESE DRAMA

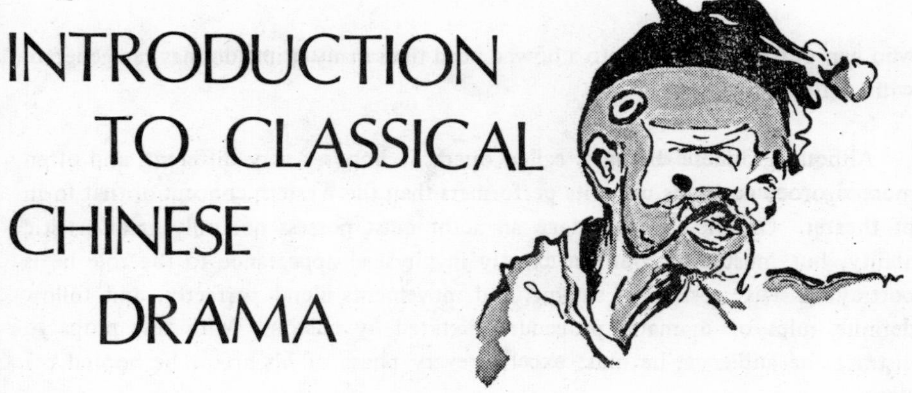

Walking into a Chinese-opera theater is like passing into another land. The actors in eye-catching regalia, the bizarre music, the unnatural singing voices—all help to bring out the full fragrance of China.

Intensely popular with every social class, this highly stylized opera unlocks the door to a deeper understanding of a race that occupies a fourth of the world's population.

To appreciate it fully, the foreigner must shed all preconceived notions he has been taught to associate with European opera. He will probably be awed by the first strident notes of music, and vaguely irritated because they cannot be forced into the kind of melodic patterns usually found in Western music. Beauty is expressed by musical scales very different from the European. The musical knowledge of the average Westerner, limited to that of his own civilization, makes it difficult for him to appreciate the subtle nuances and rich variety produced by the Chinese singers. However, once he has become accustomed to this form of art, he will accept their method of delivery as perfectly natural, correct, and spiritually moving.

Chinese opera is a feast for the eyes. Actors—some with grotesquely painted faces—storm magnificently onto the stage, their gorgeous robes emphasizing the gymnastic movements of their bodies. The female roles are performed by beauties who can put more pathos into a bowed head than many prima donnas can generate with a flood of tears.

Although Chinese drama is called opera, it imposes very different, and often more rigorous demands upon its performers than the Western concept of that form of theater. On the Chinese stage an actor must possess not only great artistic ability, but must also conform exactly in physical appearance to the role he is portraying. His costumes, singing, and movements blend perfectly, and follow definite rules of dramatic procedure dictated by custom. With few props to distract the audience, he must excel in every phase of his art or be hooted off stage.

By strict adherence to traditional rules regarding speech, song, movements, costumes, make-up, and musical accompaniment, Chinese opera achieves almost perfect harmony, a distillate of simplicity and symbolism. Disregarding historical accuracy, time, and place in their costumes, the actors do not copy life as in Western drama, but portray human emotion in an artificial mosaic of music, dance, and song. Theatergoers are usually completely familiar with the plots, finding enjoyment in the individual interpretations of famous actors.

The history of Chinese opera actually winds its way back into the dim forest of legends which grew thousands of years before Christ in the land of the "Black-Haired People."

The score for an instrument called *shao* (韶) is reputed to have been composed in the twenty-seventh century B.C. and was referred to as the greatest contribution to ancient Chinese music. Centuries afterward, when Confucius heard the music of the *shao,* he was said to be so enraptured that for three months he had no taste for meat, exclaiming, "I hardly knew that one could make music to such a state of excellence!" Unfortunately, China's ancient music has not survived in written form; we can only guess that some of what we hear today has been passed down the centuries by the musicians–who learned from their masters by ear.

The founder of the great Han dynasty, Liu Pang (劉 邦), used music to defeat his greatest rival. Hsiang Yü (項羽), army came from the kingdom of Ch'u (楚), and he had encamped them in a place far from home, which the Han army proceeded to surround. One night, Liu Pan ordered his men to sing the songs of

Ch'u. Hsiang Yü heard these songs from all sides and exclaimed, "Can the army of Han have taken Ch'u? And the men of Ch'u are so many!" Demoralized, Hsiang Yü's army was defeated, and he was killed. Liu Pang became emperor in 206 B.C.

Music had reached such importance in this land called "All That Is Under Heaven" that Han Emperor Wu (武 帝: 141-87 B.C.) created an Imperial Office of Music to control ceremonial, folk, scholarly, military, and national melodies. So exacting were the rules regarding musical performance that the responsibility for its perfection was later turned over to the Office of Weights and Measures.

Both music and choral dancing were well developed during the Han dynasty (206 B.C.-220 A.D.), when the feudal system melted away, to be replaced by a social order of gentry who had a thirst for culture and knowledge. Except for the Tartar wars and one rebellion, these were four hundred years of power and cultural growth.

The most important historical record of previous ages was compiled in the Han dynasty by Ssu-ma Ch'ien (司馬遷: 145-79 B.C.), the Father of Chinese History, and contains many detailed references to the entertainment of ancient times. In the chapter on comic characters, he writes of one Yu Meng (優孟: *circa* 610 B.C.), court jester of the kingdom of Ch'u, who was probably the first "actor" in the annals of theatrical art in China. His surname Yu in its many combinations means "a player" to this day.

When China added regions in the West to its immense territories, it imported some of the musical instruments used by the barbarians, including the *P'i P'a* (琵琶) and *hu ch'in* (胡琴), which are still heard in Chinese classical drama.

The end of the Han period marked the beginning of the division of China, and over three centuries of unrest. There was a sharp distinction between a new feudal nobility in the North, brought in by invading Turks and Mongols, and the South, where one clique after another seized power and kept the Chinese gentry alive.

After three hundred sixty years of conflict, the gentry won the upper hand over the warrior nomads of the North and China was reunited once more. However, the musical culture of the gentry had undergone many changes. The hot spice of strange music from Central Asia and the aborigine territories in the South was added to the plain salt and pepper of the older Chinese music.

The reunification of China was brought about by the Sui dynasty (589-618), which, however, soon collapsed and was replaced by the long-lived T'ang dynasty (618-906). The performing arts received a boost during the reign of T.ang Emperor Hsüan Tsung (玄 宗: 712-755). One of the most famous rulers of China, Hsüan Tsung is known to this day as "The Brilliant Emperor," or Ming Huang (明 皇). Fond of music, Ming Huang established a college known as the "Pear Garden," or *Li Yuan* (梨 園), where hundreds of young men were trained as vocalists, musicians, and dancers. In a separate school, several hundred beautiful young girls were given instruction in these arts, under the direct supervision of the Emperor. Although the resulting performances of the artists were not in the category of drama as we know it, opera actors are still called "Children of the Pear Garden."

It is said that the college was the outcome of the Emperor's journey to the moon, where he saw a troupe of skilled performers in the Palace of Jade and decided that he, too, must have entertainment in his earthly palace. However, it is much more likely that Ming Huang wanted to amuse his favorite concubine, the famed Yang Kuei-Fei (楊 貴 妃), who is the heroine of countless plays and stories. To make her perfectly formed almond eyes twinkle with mirth, the Emperor occasionally donned a clown's costume to caper around the stage with the actors. For a change, Ming Huang would listen to the seven hundred members of his court orchestras, or sit in the garden and enjoy melodies pouring forth from the outdoor orchestra consisting of over a thousand musicians and singers.

However, not until about nine hundred years ago, in the Sung dynasty (960-1126), was Chinese drama truly born. In the reign of Emperor Chen Tsung (真 宗: 998-1023), stories began to be acted out in intermissions between musical or other shows. These were at first called *tsa chü* (雜 劇), or "mixed performances." Gradually the imperial entertainers began to combine their choral dances, songs, and music with these *tsa chü*. During the Southern Sung dynasty (1127-1280), the idea of telling a story by means of dance combined with music and song became increasingly popular. This was perhaps the first real Chinese drama and was called *nan ch'ü* (南 曲), or "southern drama," because it came to bloom in the Southern Sung capital.

From legendary times, the Chinese enjoyed dancing and singing troupes along with their orchestras. When the Mongols conquered North China, there was only a limited number of what might be called "poem-music dances" as developed there in the Northern Sung and Kin dynasties; but there was also a profusion of story-tellers who sang out their tales in verse form, accompanied by simple music. The *nan ch'ü* was confined at that time to the Linan (臨 安) area, present-day Hangchow (杭 州), the Southern Sung capital.

The Mongols learned to like the storytellers, and northern Chinese scholars set to writing novels and stories in this vein, using the colloquial language, which was easier for the Mongol conquerors than the literary style. Much of this was simply the writing down of the tales with which the storytellers had been entertaining their audiences. Probably influenced by the *tsa chü* and the *nan ch'ü,* they also began to transform the tales into innumerable plays for theaters that mushroomed in almost every town and city during the period of Mongol rule. And these plays were acted out with music, dancing, and song. Thus the storytellers' art blossomed into *pei ch'ü* (北 曲), or "northern drama."

These operas were acted out all year round except during a mourning period for a deceased emperor. On temporary stages in open markets, courtyards, and palaces, actors donned magnificently gaudy costumes and employed great histrionic skill to thrill their audiences.

About fifty years after taking North China from the Kin dynasty, the Mongols conquered the Southern Sung and established Kublai Khan as the emperor of all China. During the Mongol or Yuan dynasty (1280-1367), Chinese opera was divided into these two schools, the *nan ch'ü* and the *pei ch'ü*. The most representative *pei ch'ü* of the Yuan period is *Hsi Hsiang Chi* (西 廂 記), or *The Western Chamber,* attributed to a certain Wang Shih-fu (王 實 甫), who supplied thirteenth-century audiences with several plays emphasizing romance and intrigue.

According to the story, a lady and her beautiful daughter, Ying Ying (鶯 鶯), are staying in a temple where rooms are often rented to devoted visitors. Chang Sheng (張 生), a handsome young student who is also staying in the temple, rescues the ladies from desperate robbers in the prescribed heroic fashion. In the heat of the moment, the lady promises her daughter's hand in marriage as a fitting reward. Unfortunately, when danger is gone, so is the lady's gratitude, and she withdraws her offer. By means of an intricate stratagem employed by the lady's maid, the couple are eventually united.

When Chang Sheng asked for a secret meeting with Ying Ying, he received a coy poem that has become a classic:

> *"In the moonlit night someone is waiting*
> *With the door ajar in the western room.*
> *Across the wall the flower shadows stir . . .*
> *Ah, perhaps my love is here!"*

Generations have wept and cheered over *P'i P'a Chi (*琵琶記*)*, or *The Lute,* one of the most famous *nan ch'u,* supposedly written by Kao Ming (高明) around 1350, at the end of the Yuan dynasty. Some admirers claim that *The Lute* is one of the finest Chinese plays. As lengthy as a Shakespearean play, it is arranged in as many as forty-two scenes.

Ts'ai Yung (蔡邕), so the play goes, must travel to the capital to study and get his final degree, leaving a devoted wife, Wu Niang (五娘), behind with his parents. Under political pressure, Ts'ai Yung is forced to marry the daughter of one of the emperor's ministers. He does so, singing sadly of his home and the wife he has deserted. Meanwhile, tragedy strikes the family. A terrible famine brings about the death of his parents and pitiful Wu Niang is left alone. In a heart-rending scene, she cuts off her long tresses to sell so that she will have enough funds to give the parents a proper burial. After many scenes, Wu Niang locates Ts'ai Yung and is reinstated as one of the household. Ts'ai Yung and his two wives live happily ever after. Chinese audiences are deeply touched by the filial piety displayed by Wu Niang for her in-laws and the kindly, accommodating nature of the second wife.

Under the patronage of the first emperor of the Ming dynasty (1368-1643), *nan ch'ü* increased enormously in popularity until it overshadowed the northern drama. The most energetic branch of southern drama became known as *k'ün ch'ü* (崑曲) because its roots were firmly embedded in K'ünshan (崑山), Kiangsu. It remained tops in prestige among all classical styles for close to three hundred years.

A new drama, *Ching Hsi,* or "Capital[1] Opera," took its place toward the middle of the Manchu or Ch'ing dynasty (1644-1911). Capital Opera owes its spectacular birth to the emperor Ch'ien Lung (乾隆: 1736-1795). During his long reign of sixty years, Ch'ien Lung encouraged the maintenance of theatrical troupes throughout the land. To celebrate his birthdays, the Emperor called the best operatic troupes in the country to his capital of Peking. After the festivities, many troupes stayed on in the great city to make it the center of dramatic activities.

Capital Opera is written in a simplified literary (or sometimes even a highly colloquial) style and employs features of the different drama groups that migrated to Peking from all parts of China. The folk opera (*pangtzu,* 梆子) of Shensi province contributed the use of the all-important wooden time-beater. Anhui-province troupes brought into Capital Opera the two musical scales–*erh huang* (二黃) and *hsi p'i* (西皮)–for the snakeskin fiddle (*hu ch'in,* 胡琴). However, Hupeh province has had the greatest influence–so much so that many of the lyrics of arias even today are heard in a Hupeh accent.

For the past two hundred years or more, because of early, decisive support from the Manchu court and the popularity of the actors, Capital Opera has been the outstanding form of dramatic entertainment. Not even the advent of motion pictures has dulled the resplendence of Capital Opera in the eyes of most Chinese.

Of course, there are many very vital, regional Chinese-opera styles, such as the Cantonese, the Shaohsing, the Teochiu, the Taiwanese, the Hokkien, and many others, but Capital Opera is acknowledged as the queen in all aspects: stagecraft, training of actors, acrobatics, costumes, singers, music, and art itself.

---

1. The Chinese words *hsi* (戲) and *chü* (劇) both mean "opera," or "drama." The word *ching* (京) means "capital." When the capital of China was moved from Peking (Pei-ching. 北京, or "northern capital") to Nanking (Nan-ching, 南京, or "southern capital") in 1927, the name of Capital Opera (*Ching Hsi,* 京戲) was changed to Peiping Opera (*P'ing Chü,* 平劇) after the new name of the city, Pei-p'ing (北平). However, a constantly used traditional name dies hard. In Taiwan today, the use of the term *P'ing Chü* or "Peiping Opera" is widespread, as is another name the modern generation is trying to popularize, *Kuo Chü* (國劇), "National Opera."

In Taiwan, the most professional Capital Opera troupe is *Ta P'eng* (大 鵬), which is composed of over one hundred excellent performers and musicians on the payroll of the Chinese Air Forec. Founded in 1949, *Ta P'eng* made such a unique contribution to the promotion of Capital Opera on the island that other branches of the armed forces have been inspired to follow suit and organize their own troupes. Symbolism seems to have played a role in the nomenclature of these troupes. *Ta P'eng* fits the Air Force, since *p'eng* is a "roc," a bird of enormous size; *Lu Kuang* (陸光) of the Army means "the glory of the land," *Hai Kuang* (海光), of the Navy is Chinese for "the glory of the Navy"; and *Ming To* (明駝) of the Combined Supply Service, means a fast camcl.

In addition, there are several amateur clubs, usually affiliated with some business organization. The expenses involved are mostly met from special funds set aside for entertainment purposes. Both the National Taiwan University and the National Chengchi University also have Capital Opera clubs which offer vocal training and occasionally give public performances.

Of the famous opera stars now living in Taiwan, Ku Cheng-ch'iu (顧正秋) is one who has greatly assisted the development of Capital Opera since her arrival in 1947. Her efforts and superior talent have helped to set a standard of performance far above that previously known to the residents of Taiwan.

There is a department of Chinese opera in the College of Chinese Culture. It has frequently made public performances in Taipei and Yangmingshan. Taiwan is rapidly developing its own "Pear Gardens" where aspiring young opera stars may receive proper training for careers on stage. Of the three schools, the Junior Ta P'eng, the Junior Lu Kuang, and the Foo Hsing School of Dramatic Arts *Fu-hsing:* 復興戲劇學校 *),* the last is generally recognized as the best at the present time.

Established by Mr. Wang Chen-tsu (王振祖) in the spring of 1957, the Foo Hsing school in Peit'ou(北投), a suburb of Taipei, was the first private opera school in Taiwan. Since 1968 it has been government-subsidized and has moved to Neihu and is now called National Foo Hsing Opera School. Surrounded by beautiful mountain scenery, with rehearsal rooms, offices, dining halls, classrooms, and auditorium, the school follows the traditional methods of teaching the art. The seven-year course at Foo Hsing is full of excitement and much hard work for the children, who range in age from eight to fifteen years. The day begins with a visit to a hilltop, where—with only the birds for accompaniment—they shout lustily for ten minutes. This daybreak shouting is the time-honored method of cultivating the falsetto voice essential to an opera singer. Through this uninhibited yelling, pupils increase the volume of their voices and gradually improve quality and resonance. The next step is to give the voice its color and life. Twice a day, the children take vocal lessons to the tune of the two-stringed fiddle and the meticulous tap-tap of the teacher's baton. Each singing group develops a certain style so that its members may acquire voices suitable for specific roles.

Fencing, too, is an art that both boys and girls must learn to perfection. The girls have an extra hazard when they wield the long poles, for their feet are strapped to tiny wooden shoes designed to give them the appearance of having "golden lilies" (bound feet). With such encumbrances, it requires years of strenuous practice to walk, dance, and execute gymnastics.

Since every movement is completed with ballet-like precision, acrobatic proficiency is necessary to success in all kinds of roles. Only through rigid daily drill can performers acquire a uniform beauty in their actions The movements of ill-trained performers appear so gauche that even first-rate singing cannot be expected to counterbalance this drawback.

Ordinary school subjects also are taught at Foo Hsing, with the result that students are either working on the R's or operatic skills every moment of their waking hours. Retired opera stars supervise the health, education, and talents of each student, trying to fit him into the role he will be best suited for when he graduates. Strict discipline is enforced at all times by the dormitory mothers and fathers.

There is always an atmosphere of subdued anticipation in the classrooms when the school is about to put on a full dress performance in a downtown Taipei theater. Backstage, experienced actors assist the children as they learn how to paint the operatic masks on their young faces and don resplendent costumes. When the performance is over, and each child snugly tucked into bed, the teachers carefully make notes for the future improvement of their young charges.

Besides performing locally, the Foo Hsing troupe has entertained Capital

Opera lovers in Thailand and the Philippines and is planning several overseas tours in the future. With such enthusiastic audiençes, Capital Opera is rapidly flowering in the "Pear Gardens' of Taiwan as a concrete symbol of Chinese traditional culture, treasured both at home and abroad.

FROM ENTRANCE TO EXIT

THE permanent theater developed as part of the teahouses where audiences sat and munched on watermelon seeds, sipped tea, and chatted unconcernedly while the music and action went on. There was no admission fee; the price of the refreshments covered entertainment. Theaters were originally known by the names of these teahouses.

The stage was defined by lacquered pillars with curtained exits at the right and left. One large curtain hung at the back, against which the action took place. A casually attired orchestra sat in full view on right stage to watch every gesture made by the performers and emphasize or guide the action. During the most climactic scenes, property men and relatives or friends of the actors wandered about the stage, bringing tea to the stars or observing their performances at close range.

Modern innovations have gradually been introduced. The currently used curved apron stage is equipped with a backdrop, and a few chairs and tables representing anything from a bed to a mountaintop—or chairs and tables. A drop curtain is now used to indicate the beginning or ending of a scene as well as to hide the prop men from the audience. The orchestra sits in a screened-off area to the right of the stage or in a pit below the proscenium. Unauthorized persons are not allowed to wander about the stage, actors do not drink tea during a performance, and there is a tendency to shorten the long, drawn-out sequences to give more snap to the evening's entertainment.

A view of the present-day classical stage, with the ubiquitous table-and-chair props, back and side curtains. The actors now enter and exit through the side curtains rather than the two-curtained doors at the back of the old-fashioned stage.

Like the Elizabethan stage, with a paucity of scenery and properties, the scene can be changed by the entrance or exit of characters. On the Chinese stage, the simple action of walking around may indicate that the actors have traveled thousands of miles. In *The Faithful Harlot,* Su San and Ch'ung Kung-tao travel a distance of more than two hundred miles, from Hung Tung County to Taiyuan, the capital of Shansi province, by strolling back and forth across the stage. In like fashion, the passage of years may be indicated. It is solely the responsibility of the performers to denote where the actions are taking place, whether it is in an emperor's palace, in a lady's boudoir, or on a battlefield. Since all movements are executed with ballet-like precision, any additional props would be only a hindrance to the actors.

Performers usually enter the front stage through a curtained door upstage right, which is called *shang men* (上 門) or "upper entrance," and go out through the *hsia men* (下 門) or "lower entrance," at upstage left. However, both doorways may serve as entrance or exit for all the players. An actor may exit stage right if he means to return to the place from which he came. A character entering from the upper entrance indicates he came from outside the building in which action is taking place. Players streaming in separately through both doors show that they are coming from all directions, while two who leave the stage through different exits are obviously going in different directions.

BACKSTAGE

The Greenroom is a world by itself, with its own rules and regulations obeyed by performers and workers alike. Stars are privileged to make up in small, curtained enclosures, while the other actors sit at tables in a large room where they transform their faces into the various operatic types with surprisingly few deft strokes of paint. On this sacred ground it is taboo to whistle, jest, clap hands, or establish any communication with the audience. Wardrobe men carefully fold the valuable costumes and guard them along with a conglomeration of weapons, flags, oars, and any other objects used on stage.

Presiding over the hustle and bustle of the Greenroom is a statue called "The Grand Master,' which receives daily offerings of increase to insure a successful performance. It represents T'ang Emperor, Ming Huang, the first patron of operatic performers who established the "Pear Garden."

ACTORS

There are four main types of roles: the *sheng* (生: male lead), *tan* (旦: female lead), *ching* (净: painted-face), and *ch'ou* (丑: comic). Each type is subdivided into several groups with their own particular variations. Every factor that helps an actor fit a role has been dictated meticulously by rules of long standing. A performer has studied assiduously for years to learn how to portray perfectly a certain character on stage, and usually plays that role as long as he works.

The actors of the *sheng* (male lead) group can be separated into four divisions: warriors are *wu sheng* (武 生), intellectuals are *wen sheng* (文 生), young men are *hsiao sheng* (小 生), and old men are *lao sheng* (老 生). These are not mutually exclusive categories.

Wu sheng comprise the *ch'ang k'ao* (長 靠) or *k'ao pei* (靠 背), young warriors who are vigorous in their fight, and the *tuan ta* (短 打), whose chief function is to fight without singing. Men who play the singing warrior roles must be endowed with strong physiques and deep, resonant voices. When they stride grandly on stage, wearing magnificently ornate costumes and exuding power and assurance, they present a spine-tingling picture. In heavily embroidered garments, with gaudy pennants attached to his shoulders, the warrior brandishes his weapons so convincingly that an atmosphere of real warfare permeates the theater. *Wu sheng* wear a special type of costume which customarily follows one general pattern, but is in different colors to denote personality traits and rank. For example, a general wearing a crimson *k'ao* is undoubtedly obsessed with the idea of becoming emperor and will try to attain that goal by fair means or foul. Four triangular-shaped pennants are strapped to the shoulders of military officials who have received their authority from the emperor himself. Headdresses are as varied as the costumes—the degree of elaboration in direct proportion to the importance of the wearer.

The *tuan ta* are entirely different from the *ch'ang k'ao,* since actors in this category never sing, but provoke gasps of admiration from the audience with their tumbling prowess. They wear simple clothes—form-fitting black tunics and trousers; the most distinctive feature is an outsize beret, which is always pulled down rakishly to one side.

A *tan,* female role, a rich virtuous girl   A *lao sheng,* male role, a civil official

The *wen sheng* category is made up of more peaceful, refined gentlemen. Their fame depends on their ability to sing and convey a thought to the audience with the merest quirk of an eyebrow. Since the actions are so stylized and symbolic, it is always difficult for a foreigner to appreciate fully the genius of *wen sheng* acting. A *wen sheng* scholar, in a robe of rich material and characteristic hat with stiff earflaps perched on his head, paces with great aplomb across the stage, his planned gestures establishing a perfect understanding with a knowing audience.

A *hsiao sheng* is always the young hero, who may be a poor scholar, a prince, or a bachelor about town. He captures the hearts of the ladies with his excellent singing and delicate gestures, which present an appealing mixture of manliness and gentility.

The *lao sheng,* or old man, is an important character type and often the hero in a play. He is always honest, noble, and faithful, like Ma Yi in *One Missing Head.* He may be a scholar or a general, but in his enunciation he has to be fastidiously correct—a laugh, a crescendo, or a diminuendo of his voice may win enthusiastic applause from the audience. In acting, he must possess grace and distinction. A wave of the sleeve or a finger gesture may indicate happiness or woe. Every movement he makes is more subdued and full of dignity and poise than the other character types, but he must never overdo his part.

Actors of male parts, with the exception of the *hsiao sheng,* wear beards. Everybody knows that the beard signifies age, but Chinese opera uses the beard more significantly than just to show age. It is true that a male character must be over forty before he wears a beard. But it is more so that it is the type of character that determines it. Generally a quiet and wise man wears a black, gray or white beard to befit his personality and age. Like the costume, the beard must harmonize with the different kinds of dancing movements as shown by the different ways of stroking the beard that must be exactly executed so as to give a pleasant and artistic impression on the spectator. The beard movements may be slow, violent, soft, gentle or dynamic and strong.

The beard is usually made of human hair or nylon with two iron hooks to be hung over the ears. The colors range from black to white, green to red. The black beard is for a character who is over forty, gray is for one who is over fifty, while white is for one over sixty, The red or green beard is for the very rough or

A *ch'ou*, comic role, a rich funny scholar

A *ching*, painted-faced role, a fierce general.

reckless character with a painted face and he is usually a warrior.

There are mainly four styles or shapes of beard. First, the full beard (*man jan*) in black, gray or white, is for the wealthy and powerful. It is worn by a high official or general. Second, the three-strand beard (*san jan*),is divided into three parts which may also be in black, gray or white. This three-strand beard signifies a dignified, refined and noble character. It is usually worn by a *lao sheng* or an old man. Third, the fierce warrior's beard (*cha*) is fuller and longer than a three-strand beard and has a hole to expose the mouth of the wearer, usually a painted-face warrior. The colors are red, green, purple or two-tone red and black. Fourth, the moustache (*ch'ou san*) indicates a rude or comic character. The three-long-wisps moustache is worn by comedians representing petty officials or prison guards who often blow or puff them up to arouse laughter from the audience. As in all other actions performed by the actor, different ways of touching the beard are symbolic too. Smoothing the beard, grasping it tightly, patting, fondling, tossing it over the shoulder, are all classed as beard movements and must be executed exactly.

Before the present century, there were separate dramatic troupes made up entirely of men or entirely of women. In the all-male troupes, female parts were played by youths on the Capital Opera stage, as in the Elizabethan theater. In the very few all-female troupes, even painted-face roles were played by women. Although no official edicts were promulgated against the appearance of women in stage productions it was considered improper for women to act alongside men on the same stage in Ch'ing-dynasty China.

Since the advent of the Republic in 1911 women have added their glamor to the stage by playing female parts alongside men, and there is every indication that they will continue to do so. These actresses have the unique handicap of trying to imitate the characteristics of feminity as interpreted by men.

The most popular of the six *tan* or female roles is that of the "flower," *hua tan* (花 旦), who captivates the audience with her flashing eyes and tantalizing movements. In contrast to the virtuous female types, this beauteous maiden flaunts her charms with a roguish sensuality and bewitching grace. Her costumes are gaily colored and topped with a fancy hair style adorned with sparkly brilliants.

FACIAL PAINTING

A *ching* actor, Tung Cho,
as seen in *Two Men on a String.*

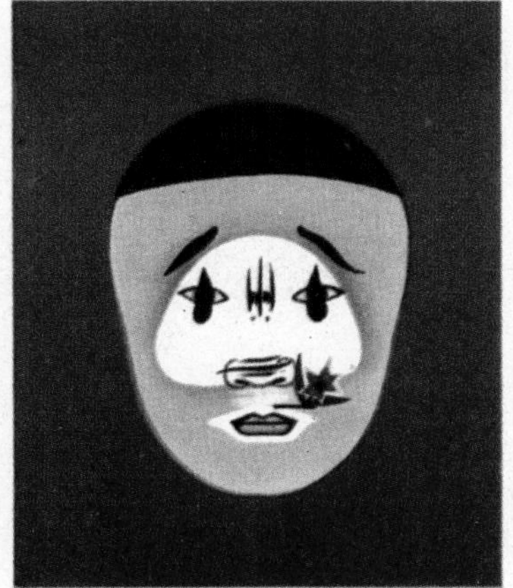

A *ch'ou* actor, Hou Hua-tsui,
in *One Missing Head.*

Grand Tutor Wen as he appears
in *One Missing Head.* A *ching* Actor.

The god of fighters, Kuan Yü,
also known as Duke Kuan,
who appears in many Capital Operas.
A *ching* actor.

Paintings by P'i Ta-ch'un

The Confucian ideal of womanhood is expressed by the *ch'ing yi* (青衣) actress, who demurely makes her entrance and takes great care to be ladylike and retiring. With graceful mincing steps and downcast eyes, she moves around the stage, manipulating her long white undersleeves with remarkable grace. With over fifty sleeve movements to choose from, she can use them to indicate a variety of emotions as well as to signal the orchestra. This righteous lady is always dressed in subdued clothing, usually featuring a long white skirt with a high-collared black tunic, and often a wide white sash.

Young, innocent girls, *kuei men tan* (閨門旦), are also clothed in simple fashion—tight-fitting jackets over trousers—as they sing roles very much like the *ch'ing yi*. Elderly, dignified *lao tan* (老旦) may be either rich or poor ladies in costumes of dark-colored silk, leaning heavily on stout canes. Plaintive but powerful singing signifies old age, and for this reason men sometimes take the role. The *ts'ai tan* (彩旦) are wicked, lowly but sometimes comic women who manage to ensnare the other characters in a web of intrigue to further their own ends. The *tao ma tan* (刀馬旦) is clever with the sword and handles acrobatic assignments like a young boy. Like the *hua tan* type, she must also wear the small wooden shoes and expertly balances on them as she wields a sword with dizzying speed in mock battle with her antagonist. Although bound feet are no longer seen in Chinese homes, the custom is so firmly rooted in Capital Opera that it remains, not so much as a reminder of the past, but more as an additional skill to be mastered by the actor.

For all *tan* characters, with the exception of *lao tan,* who appears almost without any powder or rouge, the make-up is the same. A matte-white finish is smeared on the face and neck, then accentuated with rouge that ranges in hue from a deep crimson under the eyes to a pale pink toward the jaw. Eyes are elongated and stretched upward by means of a tight band tied around the forehead.

Painted face or *ching* roles are in an entirely separate class. It is said that face painting in China can be traced back to King Lan Ling (蘭陵王) of the Northern Ch'i dynasty (550-589). Because his looks were too feminine to command respect, he painted black lines curving upward and outward on his face to suggest ferocity and bravery. Later, in the T'ang dynasty, use was made of this technique by dance performers. Face painting developed more and more over the centuries until it reached the complex art now seen in Capital Opera.

The audience in a Chinese theater knows the moment an actor steps onto the stage what kind of character he is by the facial painting: black adorns an honest, tough warrior; treachery and power are evident in an all-white one; brave and good generals have red faces; blue signifies cruelty; and a maddening mixture of all colors adorns the face of a despicable rogue. The more admirable characters have simple, dull facial painting, while the visages of more complicated individuals are covered with glossy lines and colors. The art of applying make-up must be mastered by the actor, who painstakingly puts every stroke on his own face. One false move with the brush and his whole characterization is thrown out of balance. With his face boldly painted, the *ching* actor, in built-up shoes and colorful costume, literally overshadows everyone else on stage with his flamboyant mannerisms and exploding vitality. When he opens his mouth to sing, the very walls vibrate with the force of his powerful voice.

Clowns or *ch'ou* are instantly recognized by their use of everyday language, and the white patch of paint around their eyes and noses. They are divided into military ones, who are proficient with weapons, and civilians, who can toss off jokes in a manner that convulses the audience. Portraying an endless number of rascals, buffoons, or sly philosophers, they provide comic relief in tense moments of battle or tragedy.

COSTUME

The fascinating array of colors that enliven the stage are so dazzling that few foreign onlookers take the time to discover what they mean. The costuming is actually a mixture of several different styles worn in many dynasties, with no apparent relation to reality. Historical accuracy has been sacrificed for dramatic impact and beauty. At times, the gorgeous creations seen on stage do resemble those outfits worn by officials in various periods, but, generally, costumes have been adopted for pure effect and have little connection with the past.

Confucian tradition, which prohibited a display of the body and advocated covering everything from the chin to the toes, accounts for many of the styles, especially the long sleeves, which afford ample opportunity for dramatic posturing.

The non-military roles usually have long, wide sleeves to add grace to their movements and to display their technique in manipulating them. Sleeve movement is an art in itself and is done in harmony with every head and bodily movement. The white extension of the sleeve is called the "water sleeve. Because of their lightness and whiteness, look like rippling flowing water when the actor turns and twirls them to express his different emotions. For instance, if he wants to signal the orchestra that he is about to sing, he moves his right hand, a little below the chest downward and to the right in a circular movement. With a quick turn at the wrist in front of the slightly bent right knee, he throws the sleeve backward and a little to the right as his eyes follow the sleeve and his body lean forward in harmony with the hand movement. The left hand may repeat the same movements but in the opposite direction.

Specific colors must be worn by certain characters: yellow for the imperial family; incense brown or gray for the aged; red or blue for an honest man; black for those with unpredictable tempers; and a host of other shades. Every single item from the actor's head to his feet has been dictated by the laws of Capital Opera.

SCENERY AND PROPS

Stage props are as rigidly supervised. The principal stage properties, a table and chairs–when placed in different positions–can represent a multitude of things, including a bed, emperor's throne, waiter's counter, mountain, tall building, judge's court, or high wall. A piece of black cloth painted with white lines attached to two bamboo poles will indicate a city wall, while a mountain far away may be a board painted with rocks and trees, or more likely a phrase in the libretto.

Small flags adorned with fish, surging waves, or black lines announce storms, high waves, and floods. Bits of white paper tied on a stick held by a prop man are flakes of snow that harass the movement of troops as they struggle through the huge drifts. Two flags with wheels painted on them, carried by her attendants, clearly indicate that the lady between them is riding in a chariot. Official standards and long-handled fans are symbols of high position. Imperial commands are always displayed on silk streamers. Four foot soldiers parading back and forth, carrying banners that represent thousands of men, may be an emperor's entire army.

Devils are in the air when an actor carries a burning object in his hand. A

STANDARD STAGE PROPS

High waves at sea.

Mountains.

A horse (the horsewhip).

The clouds
on which fairies ride.

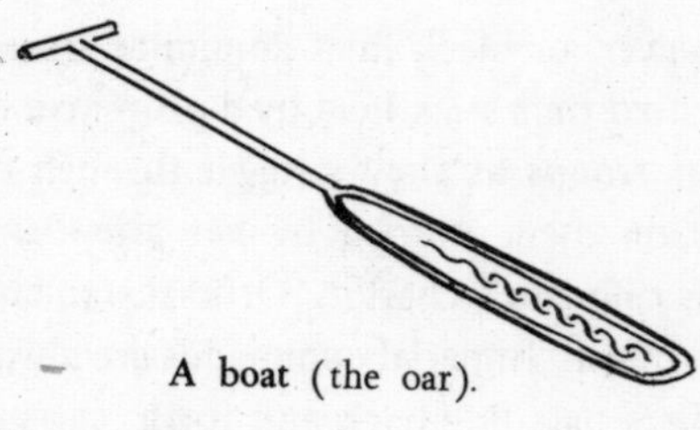
A boat (the oar).

A chariot or cart.

Drawings by Chang Ta-hsia.

STANDARD STAGE PROPS

A strongly fortified city
(the gate)

Imminent strong winds
(a black flag)

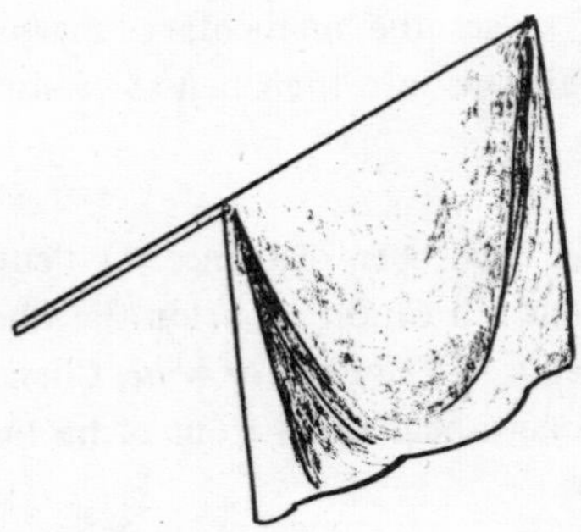

A snowstorm
(bits of paper showered
from this flag when it opened)

Drawings by Chang Ta-hsia.

duster waved about means that a ghost or fairy is nearby. When the ghost appears, he will be recognized by the wisps of white paper he has stuck around his ears.

An oar in the hands of a boatman who rocks realistically imparts the idea that he is in some kind of watercraft. When he gets out, he pushes the boat away with one foot and jumps across the invisible water onto dry land.

Many of the plays are built around ancient battles fought by cavalry, but no horses are allowed to share the limelight. Instead, a warrior will leap onto the stage waving a stick adorned with different-colored tassels. With expert mime, the rider shows how he is bucked by the skittish horse before he dismounts by flinging down the stick. After a long, hard gallop, the rider eloquently tries to persuade the horse to go on, and by the time he decides to leave his mount and walk, the audience has been made acutely aware of the horse's fatigue.

SYMBOLIC ACTION

Stepping over the threshold and opening and closing the old-fashioned double doors leading into a Chinese house are acted out with perfect mimic action. An actor simply brings his hands together to close the imaginary door, and spreads them apart to open it, carefully lifting his foot to step over the threshold. Young ladies are seen on stage tending to their sewing, but with no cloth, thread, or needles. Watching a talented actress measure out the thread, snap it between her teeth, thread the needle, and sew is as realistic as if every object were there. When she pricks her finger, everyone in the audience senses the momentary, sharp pain. In one famous scene, a farm girl herds the chickens into their pen so realistically that it is a surprise not to hear the cackling.

On the Western stage, eating and drinking have been real since the "cup and saucer" drama of T.W. Robertson of the nineteenth century, but on the Chinese-opera stage no real eating or drinking is allowed. In *The Price of Wine,* Cheng Teh only gestures to eat and drink with his right sleeve held up in front of his mouth, while his left hand guides the cup to his lips.

The gait assumed by an actor is also meaningful. A noble lady walks with grace and dignity; the flirt sways suggestively in her gaudy costume; fighters stalk; scholars pace thoughtfully; clowns scurry; and officials stride with a grand manner.

In addition, there is a particular way to sit, stand, run, fall, swim, limp, kick, stagger, slip, walk up or down a flight of stairs, scale the heights of a mountain, or glide like a ghost.

Graceful action is always coupled with perfect timing, as when the hands are moved or the long sleeves are waved about. There are 107 different hand movements that indicate a wide variety of sentiments. Every actor knows how to express himself by this intricate system of sign language.

Some normal activities are considered too vulgar for stage presentation and are altered accordingly. The act of sleeping has always been looked upon as awkward and unrefined by the Chinese, so this is never portrayed in natural position. A tired character might pretend to sleep by resting his head on his arm, but never by sprawling on the floor, chairs, or table.

SONG

Singing in its purest form with musical accompaniment can be recognized easily as singing, yet in Capital Opera the meaning of song is stretched to include more than singing. No character speaks in his natural voice, except the clown with his "laugh talk" that amuses the audience. An actor usually begins his part on stage with a *pai* (白), which is an account of himself, his situation, and perhaps his family, to make clear to the audience the episode they are about to see. This *pai* is chanted. He will chant more *pai* during the course of the play, to explain the actions on stage. Every line is cleverly rhymed according to a set of rules for rhyme and metre. The Chinese actors chant out these "spoken" lines in a rhythmic tone, the pitch and tempo depending upon the type of character and situation in the play. The monosyllabic nature of the Chinese language forces the singer to train himself to use special intonations and inflections to express a multitude of emotions. Learning the art of chanting *pai* is as difficult as learning how to sing. And the actors do learn to sing, too.

It is obvious, then, that any individual who aspires to a career on the Capital Operatic stage must submit himself to long years of strenuous practice and study unequaled in any other type of theatrics. At the end of the training period, he will have mastered the art of singing, chanting *pai*, acting, and acrobatics, and be in complete command of every movement and sound he makes.

MOUTH OF NINE DRAGONS

In an orchestra where musical notes have equations in the elements, it is no surprise that the player of the most important instrument sits in that section of the stage called the *Mouth of Nine Dragons.* No instrument may be tuned up until the little-drum player, occupying this position of honor, strikes the first note. With a *pan* (板), a kind of wooden clapper, in one hand, and a stick to beat the little drum,[1] in the other, he sets the tempo for both the musicians and the actors, and brings out the full force of string, wood-wind, brass, and percussion instruments when needed.

Capital Opera music is a mingling of mainly two styles, combined under the name p'*i huang* (皮 黃). Since music has always given life to stage effects, actors have manipulated various airs to create the atmosphere they require on stage. Different tunes indicate the emotions displayed by the actors, and are used repetitively in many plays. There is no traditional sheet music; each musician must know every melody in detail and be able to play with perfect accuracy and timing.

The *p i huang* consists of two kinds of tunes, or scales of music, the *hsi p'i* (西 皮) and the *erh huang* (二 黃). Originally the *hsi p'i* scale was used for happy, festive scenes, and the *erh huang* for sad or serious occasions, but this distinction

---

1. The little drum (*hsiao ku :* 小鼓) is technically known as the single-skin drum (*tan-p'i ku:* 單皮鼓).

PRINCIPAL MUSICAL INSTRUMENTS

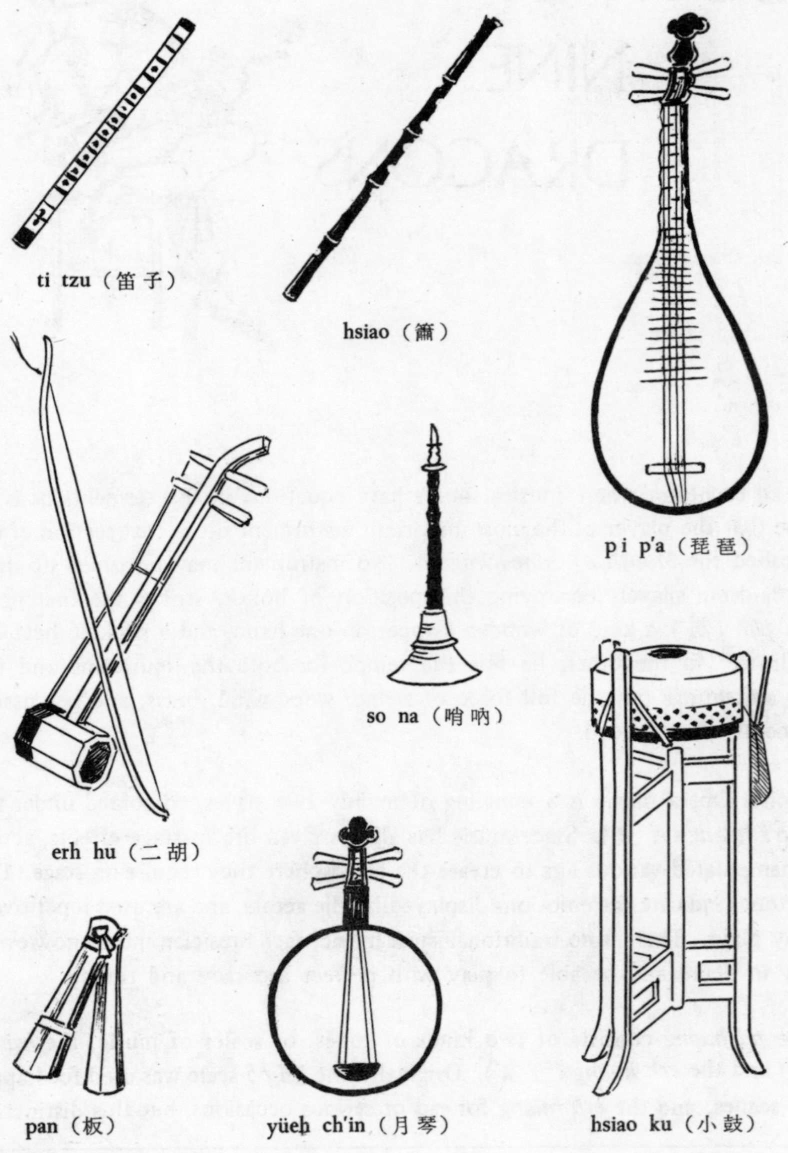

Drawings by Chang Ta-hsia.

PRINCIPAL MUSICAL INSTRUMENTS

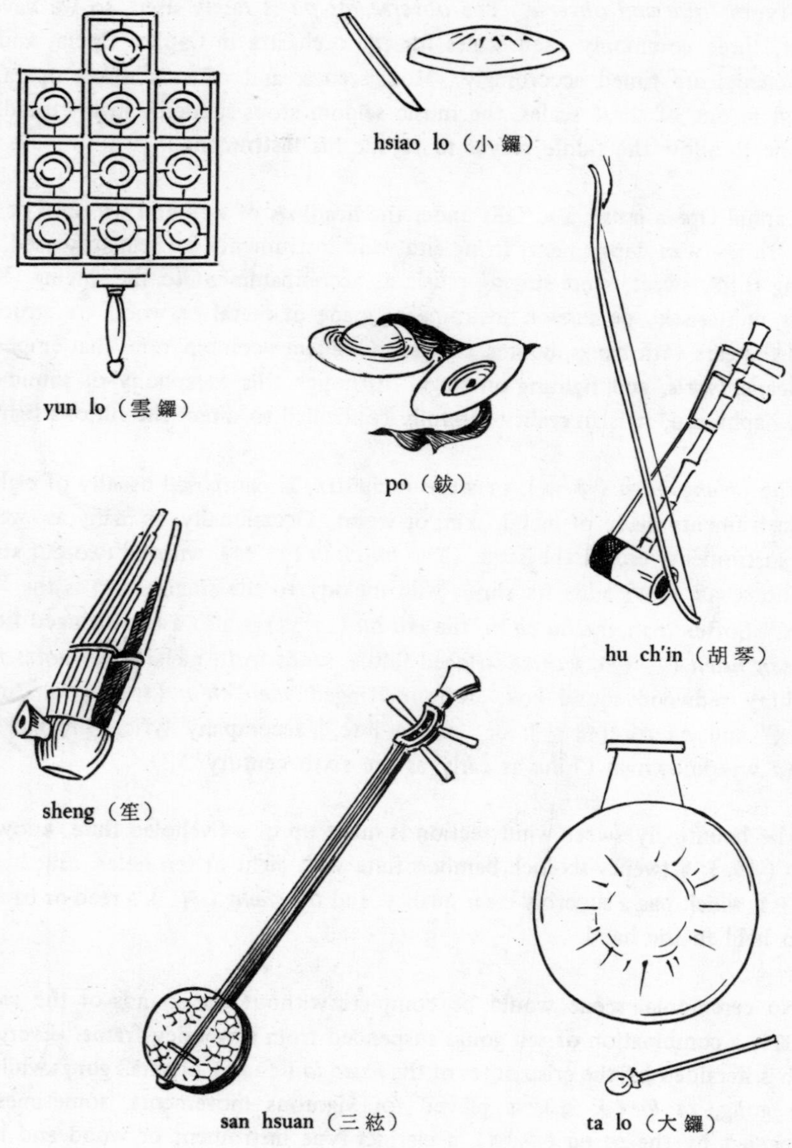

Drawings by Chang Ta-hsia.

has become blurred within the last century. Each of the two is also divided into two types: *true and obverse.* The *obverse hsi p'i* is rarely used, so we have, in effect, three commonly used scales for the orchestra in Capital Opera, and the instruments are tuned accordingly. Most scenes, and often a whole opera, are played in one of these scales; the music seldom stops suddenly in the middle of a scene to allow the fiddle player to retune his instrument.

Capital Opera music also falls under the headings of *wen* and *wu,* civil or military. In the *wen* department, string and wind instruments are primarily used, producing shrill, sweet, sense-stirring music as accompaniment to the singing. Since *wu* is militaristic, percussion instruments made of metal or wood are struck to assail the ears with bangs, booms, clangs, and raucous combinations that emphasize the leaps, twirls, and fighting on stage. Although this cacaphony of sound may seem haphazard, it is in reality carefully controlled to direct the furious fighting.

The *ch'ang mien* (場 面), or stage orchestra, is composed usually of eight to ten instruments made of metal, skin, or wood. Occasionally, as many as twenty-four instruments crowd the stage. The *hu ch'in* (胡 琴), with its two gut strings and horsehair bow, adds its shrill, wild melody to the singing and is the "first violin." Softer than the *hu ch'in,* the *erh hu* (二 胡) is also a two-stringed fiddle. The *san hsien* (三 絃), a three-stringed fiddle, sends forth melancholy notes from its shiny redwood sound box. A four-stringed *yueh ch'in* (月 琴), or "moon guitar," and *p'i p'a* (琵 琶), or "melon lute," accompany lyrical singing. The *p'i p'a* was known in China as early as the sixth century A.D.

The hauntingly sweet wind section is made up of a fiveholed flute, known as *hsiao* (簫); a twenty-six-inch bamboo flute with eight or ten holes, called *ti tzu* (笛 子), which has a superbly clear quality; and the *sheng* (笙), a reed or bamboo organ held in the hand.

No ceremonial scene would be complete without the sounds of the *yün lo* (雲 鑼), a combination of ten gongs suspended from a wooden frame. Every *tan* actor is heralded by the crisp notes of the *hsiao lo* (小 鑼), or small gong; while the large gong, *ta lo* (大 鑼), is played for vigorous movements, sometimes accompanied by the *so na* (哨 吶), a clarinet-type instrument of wood and brass. When an emperor appears, small cymbals called *po* (鈸) are clanged together. These are also used for ceremonial scenes in several plays.

Actors and orchestra work so closely together that a musician knows by the tone of his voice when the performer is about to stop, exit, or break into a roaring song. They are a team with one thought in mind: to present a perfect aural and visual interpretation of the human emotion they are portraying.

ON STAGE

A general understanding of certain features of ancient China may lead to a better appreciation of Capital Opera. First, it must be remembered that the government of ancient China was a monarchic one, ruled by the emperor, who was appointed by the will of heaven. He was also commander-in-chief of the armed forces, nominal supervisor of religious and ceremonial affairs, and administrator of justice to the state. Thus, high officials such as Wang Chin-lung in *The Faithful Harlot* and the Grand Tutor in *One Missing Head* acted for the emperor.

Appointment to official posts was made by means of competitive literary examinations held once every three years in the capital, to which candidates flocked from every part of the country. These examinations were open to all suitably qualified candidates, rich and poor alike (as are the present civil-service examinations held annually in Taipei), and it was the ambition of every young scholar to succeed and make a name for himself. The young scholar journeying to the capital for the examinations is a theme which occurs in a number of plays. Of the five plays in this book, *One Missing Head, Twice a Bride,* and *The Faithful Harlot* make use of this theme with its background of government.

Criminals were punished for their misdemeanors by decapitation, flogging, or other tortures, often symbolically represented on stage. Women prisoners were marched to the courts with a wooden kind of trap secured around their necks. The trap was a portable stocks, which fits over the shoulders so that the head could be locked in one opening and the hands in another On stage the trap is an attractive fish-shaped silver object decorated in a rather gay manner. In *The Faithful Harlot,* Su San looks quite fetching and not the least bit uncomfortable in her wooden collar as she is accused of murdering her master.

"A WIFE IS SOUGHT FOR HER VIRTUE, A CONCUBLINE FOR HER BEAUTY."

It was an established social practice–originally sanctioned as a means of securing male heirs–for a gentleman to acquire several concubines in addition to his wife. Concubines became members of the family and were subject to the supervision of the first wife, as in the case of Su San in *The Faithful Harlot.* Concubines, as exemplified by Tiao Ch'an in *Two Men on a String,* have been known to exert considerable influence on affairs of state, as well as being famed in story and legend for their beauty and charm.

Generally speaking, women occupied a secondary position in society. A woman was expected to be modest, chaste, and loyal to her husband, as portrayed by the *ch'ing-yi* characters in Capital Opera. A widow rarely married since it was considered an act of virtue to remain faithful to a dead husband, to whom she forever belonged. Few women dared violate this convention, but Mistress Yao, the widow in *One Missing Head,* not only is the murderess of her husband but the paramour of her neighbor. In those days, about the only way a wife could be rid of a husband she despised was to slip poison in his noodles or have him quietly stabbed. However, for the men it was different. Under the guise of strengthening the family line, they acquired as many concubines as they could afford.

"FILIAL PIETY MOVES HEAVEN AND EARTH"

Filial piety begets loyalty as brotherliness begets friendliness. If a man repected, loved, and obeyed his parents, it followed that he would be loyal to others entitled to their loyalty. The family is the foundation of Chinese society, and filial piety is subordinate. A son's prime allegiance is to his parents and the spirits of his ancestors.

"IN BED, HUSBAND AND WIFE; OUT OF BED, GUESTS."

There was a constant stress on ceremony and the observance of an etiquette designed to cover all aspects of daily living. Ranks of society were distinguished by the clothes worn and the types of weapons used. There were standard forms of address between superiors and inferiors. The seating of host and guests was bound by formal rules. For example, when two characters facing the audience are sitting on stage, the more superior guest always sits on the left of the stage, with the host on the right and a table separating them. When there are three officials sitting on the stage, the superior sits in the center, in front of the table, with the first subordinate on his left and the second on his right, as in Scene Four of *Twice a Bride.*

"EVERY SECT HAS ITS TRUTH AND EVERY TRUTH ITS SECT."

The Chinese are innately a tolerant race and have always allowed different religions to exist side by side. In Taiwan today, Protestant and Catholic churches are built next to Buddhist temples or Moslem mosques.

From early times Confucianism provided a system of ethics for the conduct of living, rooted in ancestor worship. As a faith, it set the whole pattern for family life and politics, as mentioned several times by Tiao Ch'an in *Two Men on a String* and by Ma Yi's daughter in *One Missing Head.* Buddhism appealed to the Chinese through its conception of life after death. A philosophy of "nonexistence," taught by Lao-tzu about the end of the fifth century B.C., evolved into a religious formula called Taoism, which later promoted spirit worship and competed with Buddhism for the religious adherence of the common people. The appearance of the god of happiness in *Twice a Bride and* the ghost in *One Missing Head* are sprinklings of Taoism. These elements of a religious nature are mixed into Capital Opera to add dramatic impact rather than to spread religious propaganda.

"ALWAYS PLEASANT AT HOME; FAR AWAY IT IS UNPLEASANT"

Old Chinese cities were surrounded by high walls whose gates were closed at nightfall, so a piece of black cloth painted with white lines to symbolize brick walls and the city gate is often used on stage. Streets were unlit and people who went out of doors after dark had to carry lanterns. The judge in *The Faithful Harlot* carries a lantern (unlit) to signify that it is night when he goes to inspect the prison. Houses were built with a threshold several inches high, which made it necessary to lift the foot when entering and departing. This accounts for the way actors always step high over the imaginary threshold on stage. Lights inside houses shone through opaque paper covering the windows, except where an inquisitive finger had poked a hole for the curious eye to peek through. This action is often mimed by a snoopy old crone in Capital Opera.

"THE IGNORANT BELIEVE WHAT THEY ARE TOLD, NOT WHAT THEY SEE."

The plays of Capital Opera are simple in structure. Puns, doggerel, and salacious jokes abound in the dialogue. Military plays describe historical episodes in which famous characters rush about the stage to engage in battles or lead whole armies into the fray.

The literature in Capital Opera is a flimsy and insufficient art. It is art for the masses, who do not care for nor understand high-sounding rhetoric. It consists mostly of everyday speech, which has been scorned by traditional scholars as vulgar. At first, there were not even written scenarios. Very little effort was made to employ flowery words in the operatic script; the attraction lies in its interpretation by talented actors. Chinese audiences delight in the folksy humor of the dialogue, dotted with popular regional jokes and references to well-known stories. They hunger for plays describing the escapades of beautiful concubines, suffering virtuous maidens, daring heroes, gods and goddesses, demons, ghosts, dragons, and capricious monkeys. Capital Opera provides them all, in brilliant and fascinating productions that manipulate reality to enhance the impression of human emotion purely expressed.

The episodic nature of Capital Opera makes it possible to lift out famous scenes from different plays and assemble them for an evening's entertainment, with the star making his appearance usually during the last hour. Onlookers arrive late, wander in and out of the theater, and settle down in their seats to see only the most important scene featuring their favorite actor. At times, several excerpts are presented, or perhaps two short plays–the choice of passages following no set rule.

In the English translation of the five operas in this book, very seldom is an indication of an aria given; only when the language or action seems to call for it have such remarks as "sings" or "singing" been inserted between the lines of the plays. No distinction is made in the English version between *pai* and actual singing, although they are clearly demarcated in the Chinese original. The reason for this is that Chinese songs usually rhyme, or at least have a rhythm which is almost impossible to duplicate in English without warping the meaning too drastically. The net effect of this translation, then, is to transform a Chinese libretto for an opera into an English play. Each of these Capital Operas naturally has suffered in this process, but the plots have emerged in stark clarity. Perhaps this is not the best way to present this Chinese art to a foreign reader–but let him judge for himself.

The translations that follow are merely the bones onto which the actor must build the flesh of his art, aided by costumes and music. However, reading the dialogue might tempt the reader to seek out a fuller understanding of this great art called Capital Opera, and will certainly give him a taste of the culture and customs of the Chinese people.

THE FAITHFUL HARLOT

(Yü T'ang Ch'un)

This play describes the eventual triumph of virtue, the virtue in this case being the faithfulness of a woman to a man. And with typical Chinese insight, *The Faithful Harlot* demonstrates that the heroine who can best dramatize this theme is a prostitute. The popularity of *The World of Suzie Wong,* which delineates the same theme in somewhat the same manner in a modern setting, seems to bear out this thesis. *Suzie* also introduced to foreigners the broad-minded Chinese concept of man-woman relationships which is so evident in this play.

To reinforce the moral of the story, an unfaithful woman is woven into the plot and, not surprisingly, meets disaster.

The Chinese name, *Yü T'ang Ch'un* (玉堂春), literally means "The Joyful Hall of Jade," a title of analogy: the hero had built a pavilion in the pleasure garden for Su San, the herione, and called it "Hall of Jade," also conferring the same name on Su San, thoughtfully adding "Joyful" when calling her by this pet name.

This is the complete play, although the eight original scenes (some are brief and nonessential) have been condensed to four. Two parts of this play are especially popular and often performed separately under the titles *Su San Is Sent to the Provincial Capital* and *Three Officials Hold Court*.

As with all popular Capital Operas, the libretto of *The Faithful Harlot* has been polished by many generations of theatergoers who have insisted that the actors skip boring passages which were intended to explain changes in heart or actions not in character with the personality of the player as first revealed. The Chinese audience would rather imagine such thought processes and get on to the dramatic confrontations or hilarious situations which hold one's attention. Under the circumstances, a brief description of the story background may help the reader

Su San is sold to a brothel, where she falls in love with a rich young scholar, Wang Chin-lung, who spends all his money for her pleasure. Penniless, Wang is turned out by the brothel-keeper, but is aided by the faithful Su San, who gives him money to journey to Nanking, the capital–to take the government examination and make his fortune. Later, she is forced to become a concubine to Shen Yen-lin, whose wife regards the younger woman as a threat to her position. The wife plans to murder Su San, but her husband unwittingly eats the poisoned noodles and dies. Of course, Su San is accused of murder, tried, and condemned. At that time it was customary to send prisoners convicted of grave offenses to a higher official for retrial. Our play begins with Su San and her guard traveling from Hung Tung County to Taiyüan, the capital of Shansi province.

This English version was first produced in Elizabeth City, South Africa, in May, 1964. It was produced again by the Grand Hotel Drama Guild, an amateur international drama group in Taipei, in July, 1968. Although no music was employed, the reading of the script itself, in addition to the authentic colorful costumes and stylized movements, provided an excellent evening of entertainment to a full-house Chinese and Western audiences.

THE FAITHFUL HARLOT
Characters

SU SAN . . . . *the heroine*
(蘇　三)

CH'UNG KUNG-TAO,
or JUSTICE. . . . . *the escort guard in charge of Su San*
(崇公道)

WANG CHIN-LUNG . . . . *the hero*
(王金龍)

SAN LANG. . . . . *Su San's pet name for Wang Chin-Lung*
(三　郎)

P'AN PI-CHENG
(潘必正)

. . . . *two judges in court*

LIU PING-YI
(劉秉義)

PRISON WARDEN . . . .*(a woman)*

MAGISTRATE WANG. . . . . *county official who first sentenced Su San*
(王縣令)

MISTRESS P'I . . . . *first wife to the merchant who purchased Su San*
(皮　氏)

CHAO CHIEN-SHENG . . . . *Mistress P'i's lover*
(趙監生)

CH'UN CHIN. . . . . *maid servant to Mistress P'i*
(春　錦)

COURT OFFICIALS AND GUARDS

SCENE ONE

On the road to Taiyüan It is open country with tree-covered hills. A chair, turned sideways, representing a rock, is on the left stage. The actors cover miles by simply walking around the stage.

Enter from up stage right, Ch'ung Kung-Tao, *or* JUSTICE. *the escort guard who is in charge of taking the prisoner* Su San *to Taiyüan for retrial. He is a kindly old man, short and stocky, with a small white beard. He is a comic character with a kind, generous heart.*

Su San *is a beautiful girl of 18, in a red jacket and trousers.*

A wooden trap has been fastened around her neck, and her hands are chained to it. This contraption was worn only by female prisoners who had committed serious crimes.

JUSTICE:

Ah ha!
You say you are right,
And I say I am right,
But who is really right?
Only heaven knows!
I, Justice Ch'ung,
Am an escort guard
Of Hung Tung County.
Today I am ordered
To take the prisoner
Su San to Taiyüan
For retrial.
Off we go!
Off we go!

Starts walking.

SU SAN:

Ai-Ya! I, Su San,
Out of Hung Tung County,

Come into the street.
Not a word is uttered,
My heart is fettered!
Oh, gentlemen!

Kneeling, downstage center.

Hear me, I pray!
Whoever goes to Nanking,
Tell my beloved San Lang
That Su San will die.
Till we meet again .
San Lang, farewell!

JUSTICE:

Why are you kneeling here in the street? Are you praying to heaven for mercy, or are you begging for traveling expenses?

SU SAN:

I am neither praying to heaven nor begging for traveling expenses. Dear Lao Po,[1] please ask whether anyone here is going to Nanking.

JUSTICE:

Why?

SU SAN:

So that I can ask him to take word to my beloved San Lang.

JUSTICE:

Still thinking of her lover.

To the audience:

Gentlemen, look at this girl—still faithful to her lover! This should teach you that if you go to a house of prostitution, you are sure to get your money's worth!

To Su San:

All right, I'll ask for you.

Yelling, to left and right.

---

1. Lao Po—a respectful term, literally meaning "old uncle."

Hey, is anyone going to Nanking?

A VOICE:

Off stage.

They all left three days ago.

JUSTICE:

Is anyone there now?

THE VOICE:

Now there are only people going to the Lama Temple in Chang Chia Pass to buy camels.

JUSTICE:

Coming back to Su San:

Did you hear what they said? There is no one going in the direction of your lover.

SU SAN:

It is said Loyang is full of flowers, yet people who are shut in prison do not even realize it's spring.

Sighs, gets up and starts walking.

Sorrowfully I walk out of Hung Tung County.

Justice *stops walking.*

Lao Po, Why are you stopping?

JUSTICE:

It's so hot! Phew! I have a stick to support me and I'm exhausted! Look at you, weighted down with a trap and heavy chains. How can you stand it? Let me take those chains off for you!

SU SAN:

Oh, no, this is the law of the court. How can you do anything about it?

JUSTICE:

Out here, who cares about the law! Outside the city, my word is law! Come, let me take them off for you.

SU SAN:

Thank you. I can see that you, Lao Po, are a very kind-hearted man.

JUSTICE:

I'm kind-hearted all right, but I haven't even got a son of my own![2]

SU SAN:

Ai-ya! How is it that such a good man like you doesn't even have one son?

JUSTICE:

Well, not having a son isn't such a bad thing, but I won't have a grandson, either!

SU SAN:

Lao Po, if you think I am good enough, I am willing to be your adopted daughter. How do you like that idea?

JUSTICE:

Oh, that's impossible. How can I ever accept such a great honor?

SU SAN:

Kneels and pushes Justice *down on the chair (a rock).*

Father, please accept the greetings of your daughter!

JUSTICE:

Now, now! Stand up.

Su San *gets up.*

Ai-ya! What a charming daughter!

Stands up.

Now, I don't have to worry any more! My adopted daughter will give me money to spend. I'll buy a fur jacket to wear . . .

Gestures to show he is well dressed.

and I'll ride in a sedan-chair. I'll play mahjong every day. People will look at me and ask, 'Who is that wealthy man?" And then I say, "I am the adopted father of so-and-so!" Ha! Ha! Just to think of it tickles me to death! At the moment, I have only one possession—this stick! Accept it as a ceremonial gift from your adopted father.

---

2. According to the old Chinese tradition, a good man was usually blessed with sons and grandsons.

Gives the stick to Su San.

Take this and use it; three legs make for lighter walking than two. Let s go slowly!

SU SAN:

Thank you, father. Let's go.

They continue to walk around the stage and stop with one on either side of stage.

Ah, poor me! When I was Yü T'ang Ch'un, the famous sing-song girl, how beautifully dressed I was! Now look at me–in this prisoner's skirt and blouse. I hate my cold-hearted parents! For the love of money, they sold me to a house of prostitution!

JUSTICE:

Ho, you are angry with your parents for selling you to a house of prostitution! They had their reasons for doing so . . . what else could they do . . . as poor as they were? I'm sure it was the last resort. No use blaming them. So take it easy now and stop worrying. When you come to think of it, it's much better to be a prostitute than a homeless streetwalker! Let s walk on.

SU SAN:

Yes, let's walk on.

They start to walk and stop after they have changed sides.

And cursed be that merchant of Shansi, Shen Yen-lin! He had no right to buy me from the house of prositution!

JUSTICE:

Ai, this shows how ungrateful you are! Shen yen-lin was kind enough to spend much money to free you from prostitution. How can you blame him for such generosity? Tsk! Tsk!

Pause.

Strictly speaking, he wasn't entirely in the right, With one wife already, why did he take you home with him? How could he expect to squeeze two donkeys into one stable? Besides, you are much more beautiful–much younger–than the other wife. Naturally, the old man wanted to spend all his time with you. That, of course, painted the first wife s eyes green with envy!

SU SAN:

Let's go on.

They walk and stop again.

Third, cursed be that first wife Mistress P'i, for her wickedness and cruelty! She shouldn't have put poison in the noodles to kill her husband.

JUSTICE:

Do you really blame her for that? It was only natural for her to do such a thing. After all, with you in the house, what was her position? Her only way to get back into her husband's favor was to get rid of you. That old fool, Shen Yen-lin, ate the poisoned noodles by mistake. So let this be a warning to all you gentlemen . . . .

Addresses the audience:

To consult with your wife before buying a concubine!

SU SAN:

We'd better go on.

They walk and then stop again.

Fourth, cursed be that hateful girl, Ch'un Chin. She should never have plotted with Chao Chien-sheng to help Mistress P'i.

JUSTICE:

Why–she's only a slave girl! Naturally, she would obey Mistress P'i, the woman who bought and reared her. How can you expect her to be on your side?

Pause.

Frankly speaking, though, that girl has never been good or decent. She always wears too much powder and rouge. Every evening she used to prance out of the house–gaudily dressed–to flirt with all the young men. I don't blame the men. Old as I am–when she rolled those eyes at me the other day–my heart beat twice as hard! Dammit! I'm too old for that kind of thing.

SU SAN:

Let's walk on.

They continue to walk around thc stage and stop again.

Fifth, cursed be that corrupt Magistrate Wang!

JUSTICE:

So you hate Magistrate Wang, too! How unreasonable! Throughout the ages, government officials have always tried to accumulate great wealth. It's only the fault of fate that you happened to meet a corrupt one.

SU SAN:

Sixth, cursed be those guards in the court who shared the bribe.

JUSTICE:

Su San, the more you talk, the less sense you make! Since most officials take bribes, you can't blame us guards for taking a few tips! Now–look at these shoes of mine. Did they appear out of thin air? No, I had to buy them. Who gave me the money?

You are a smart girl–I'm sure you can figure that out for yourself. It is said a person lives on his trade and station in life. How can you curse us for taking money? If you want us to be honest, the best way is not to file suits in court. All right, let's walk on.

They continue to walk and then stop.

SU SAN:

Seventh, cursed be the one who tortured me to confess to the murder.

JUSTICE:

Su San, you don't understand. Since the official had already taken the bribe, he became nervous and didn't know how to handle the case unless you admitted your crime. So if you wouldn't confess freely, he had to torture you. As for the one who did the actual torturing, he was just obeying orders! Come along!

They walk again and then stop.

SU SAN:

Eighth, cursed be that Tiger Li, who forced me to confess to the crime. Ai-ya! Curse this and curse that! There isn't a single good person in Hung Tung County!

JUSTICE:

Greatly offended, he walks toward Su San.

What! Isn't there one good person in Hung Tung County? Are you including me? All right, come, come, come! Put these chains back on! How ungrateful you are!

SU SAN:

Aside, with her hand raised on one side and with the other hand points to Justice.

A word carelessly spoken aroused the anger of my father. Let me humor him with some sweet, comforting words.

To Justice:

Father, please forgive me. Of course, there isn't a person in the whole empire as fine and virtuous as you are!

Caresses his chest.

My dear father, you are the kindest person in the whole wide world!

JUSTICE:

Laughing–

Ha! Ha! The stroking of her small hand on my chest and the sweet sounds coming from her lips have completely driven my anger out into the sea. All right, my dear daughter, I am not angry any more. Let's go on.

They walk a step or two, then stop.

Oh! Oh! I see that Taiyüan is not far away now. I'd better put back the trap and chains.

SU SAN:

Father dear, because I have been gravely wronged, a friend in jail wrote a petition for me, requesting the high officials in Taiyüan to set me free. I have hidden it beneath my blouse, next to my body. Please tell me how I can be sure this petition will reach the hands of the high officials.

JUSTICE:

Ummm, let me see. Yes, there is a way. Put it inside the locking device of the trap. When the trap is taken off, the paper will fall out. The high officials will surely see it then.

SU SAN:

Thank you, father.

Justice locks the trap and chains on Su San.

We must be careful now .... we are close to Taiyüan. I wonder what will happen to me. Will I be executed . . . or . . . will I be freed?

Weeps.

Su San *and* Justice *go out to upstage left.*

SCENE TWO

This is the trial scene. The prop man enters to arrange the chairs and tables. Everything is placed in a dignified and symmetrical manner. In the center of the stage there are three tables, with three chairs behind them. These are the seats for the high officials gathered in Taiyüan, the capital of Shansi province. Wang Chin-lung, *who has now become a high central government official, seats himself in the center. Two other judges,* Liu Ping-yi *and* P'an Pi-cheng, *sit on his right and left. Four guards, two on each side, stand in front of the table near the front stage.*

CHIN-LUNG:

I, Wang Chin-lung, have been ordered by His Imperial Majesty to inspect eight courts of Shansi. I have been to three counties, and Hung Tung was the fourth. Since arriving in Taiyüan, I have been busily reading criminal cases from that county. The most interesting is the husband murder case. I'll take that one up first. There'll be absolute justice in my court.

To the two judges:

Honorable judges, I want you to help me see that the imperial laws are strictly obeyed. No amount of tears or influence will be allowed to twist the truth.

To the guards:

Bring in the prisoner.

A guard exits to upstage right and returns with Justice *and* Su San, *who is in heavy chains.*

SAN:

Aside.

Here I am, in the court of the capital. When I look up, all I can see are glistening swords and daggers. How frightening! I feel like a fish caught in a net. Woe is me! Oh, how bitter is my life!

Weeps as she walks in.

Justice *leads her before the three high officials and they both kneel.*

JUSTICE:

My name is Ch'ung Kung-tao, or Justice. I am an escort guard for the prisoner Su San. My greetings, honorable judges.

CHIN-LUNG:

Prisoner, raise your head.

SU SAN:

Lifting her head–

Thank you, Your Honor.

CHIN-LUNG:

Astonished. Aside, with raised sleeve.

Ai-ya! So this prisoner turns out to be my Su San! Oh, all of a sudden I feel dizzy . . . it gets darker . . . and darker . . .

He faints, and slumps over the table.

P'AN PI-CHENG:

The courtroom will be cleared!

All except Chin-lung *exit to the left,* Justice *and Su* San *to the right. A guard enters from the left, leading in a doctor. The doctor comes up to the table, examines* Chin-lung, *gives him some medicine, and exits to the left.* Chin-lung *recovers consciousness.*

CHIN-LUNG:

Out of the fog and clouds I came back to consciousness. Let me raise my head to look . . . ah . . . with blurred vision .. .

GUARD:

Wake up, Your Honor.

CHIN-LUNG:

Aside.

The court will come to order!

Enter the judges, Liu *and* P'an, *and guards. They all resume their places.*

P'AN:

What was wrong? Is is an old trouble or a new disease?

CHIN-LUNG:

It was the recurrence of an old disease!

P'AN:

You certainly gave us all a fright!

CHIN-LUNG:

Thank you both for your kind consideration.

P'AN:

Shall we continue to question the prisoner?

CHIN-LUNG:

Of course! Since this is a serious murder case, how could we let it pass lightly?

P'AN:

Your Honor, you are kind to the people—as kind as a father to his children. All right, let us proceed to question the prisoner. Guards, bring in the murderess.

GUARD:

Walks to the right, facing the entrance, and calls loudly—

Bring in the murderess.

Justice *and* Su San *enter from the right.*

SU SAN:

Kneels

Greetings to Your Honors.

CHIN-LUNG:

Do you have a petition?

SU SAN:

Yes, Your Honor.

CHIN-LUNG:

Present it,

SU SAN:

I can't, Your Honor!

CHIN-LUNG:

What? When I ask if you have a petition, you say, "Yes," Now you say you can't show it to me. It's obvious you are a cunning and vicious woman. Gentlemen, order them to flog her!

P'AN:

Guards, flog her!

The guard approaches Su San *and is about to whip her.*

SU SAN:

Ai-ya! Your Honor, have mercy on me! I haven't yet finished what I started to say.

GUARD:

Then hurry up and say it!

SU SAN:

My three honorable judges, I assure you I am innocent. My husband's first wife, Mistress P'i, caused me to be condemned to death by bribing officials. Before I was transferred here for a retrial, a kind man who was also in jail wrote a petition to plead for my release. Fearing Mistress P'i might have it seized, I hid the petition inside the wooden trap. Have mercy on me! Open the trap at once! If you will only read the petition, I shall be content to close my eyes[3] when I die! Ai-ya! Ai-ya! Woe is me!

She cries.

P'AN:

Turning to Chin-lung–

Your Honor, may I ask if we can pardon her from flogging?

CHIN-LUNG:

Pardon her, then.

P'AN:

Open the trap at once!

JUSTICE:

Yes, Your Honor, let me open the trap.

He opens the trap for Su San.

P'AN:

Justice, you may go now, but come back in three days for the verdict.

Justice *exits to the right.*

CHIN-LUNG:

Prisoner, describe your past life.

SU SAN:

Your Honor, allow me to begin at the beginning. I, Yü T'ang Ch'un, am now kneeling before you.

CHIN-LUNG:

Tsk! Tsk! On the petition it says Su San, not Yü T'ang Ch'un. You are indeed a cunning woman!

GUARD:

Shall I flog her, Your Honor?

---

3. In China, it was believed that a person who had been wronged would not close his eyes in death.

P'AN:

Just a moment.

SU SAN:

Weeps. Turns to Chin-lung–

Please . . . Your Honor . . .

P'AN:

Sensing the past relationship between the prisoner and his senior–

Guards, withdraw.

The four guards go out, two to the left and two to the right.

Prisoner, turn around and kneel, facing the door.

Su San *turns around with her face toward the audience.*

Now, prisoner, take your time and relate the reason for calling yourself Yü T'ang Ch'un.

SU SAN:

Yü T'ang Ch'un is the name given to me by a young scholar with whom I am deeply in love.

P'AN:

How old were you when you first became a sing-song girl?

SU SAN:

The procuress bought me when I was exactly seven;

P'AN:

How long did you stay in the house of assignment?

SU SAN:

Nine years.

LIU PING-YI:

Since you were sixteen, you were old enough to know about love. Who was your first lover?

P'AN:

Yes, who was your first lover?

SU SAN:

When I was sweet sixteen, I had a blissful and happy time. I fell in love with Wang . . .

P'AN and LIU:

Eagerly.

Wang who? What was his given name?

SU SAN:

Ah . . . Wang is a nobleman.

P'AN:

What kind of man is this Master Wang?

LIU:

Yes, what kind of man is he?

SU SAN:

It is said he was the third son of a high official on the Board of Civil Offices.

CHIN-LUNG:

Stop! This court is inquiring into the case of a murdered husband! Who wants to hear about your love affairs in a house of prostitution?

P'AN:

Ah, Your Honor, the husband murder case must be investigated thoroughly.

CHIN-LUNG:

I agree with that.

LIU:

And the love affairs of the people involved must also be looked into.

CHIN-LUNG:

Uncomfortably.

All right . . . the love affairs must be looked into? Proceed to question.

LIU:

Proceed!

CHIN-LUNG:

Embarrassed.

This . . . uh . . .

He laughs bitterly, while P'an *and* Liu *follow him in laughter.*

SU SAN:

The first time he came to the house, he gave three hundred ounces of silver for only a cup of jasmine tea and left without saying a word.

P'AN:

He must have been a very generous man!

CHIN-LUNG:

He was certainly noble!

LIU:

How can you say he was generous and noble? I think it is unfortunate for the House of Wang to have such a disgraceful son to ruin the family!

Wang Chin-lung *smiles ironically while the two judges laugh heartily.*

CHIN-LUNG, P'AN, and LIU:

Proceed!

SU SAN:

The second time the young scholar came to the house, he brought thirty-six thousand ounces of silver.

P'AN and LIU:

How long did he stay in the house?

SU SAN:

After he stayed in the house for less than a year, he had spent all his thirty-six thousand ounces of silver like ashes.

LIU:

All that silver gone within one year?

P'AN:

Did you serve his food on silver plates and clothe him in silver?

SU SAN:

But I had expenses!

CHIN-LUNG:

That's right! She had expenses.

LIU:

Your Honor, how do you know she had expenses?

CHIN-LUNG:

Flustered.

Ah . . . how do I know?

LIU:

Yes, how do you know?

CHIN-LUNG:

Her accounts are listed in the petition.

LIU: So! Her accounts are listed, eh?

CHIN-LUNG:

Yes, they are listed there–in black and white!

P'AN:

If that is the case, let us look into her personal accounts!

CHIN-LUNG;

Yes, let's . . .

Shows uneasiness and displeasure; P'an *and* Liu *laugh.*

P'AN, LIU, and CHIN-LUNG:

Proceed!

SU SAN:

I first bought some gold cups and a jade basin, then a jade tray and bottle. The south building and the north building were erected by the young scholar, and he also had a beautiful pavilion built called the Pavilion of a Hundred Blossoms.

P'AN and LIU:

After the young scholar spent so much money for the house, how did the procuress treat him?

SU SAN:

That cursed woman is cold-blooded and cruel. In the heart of winter, she turned him out into the wind and snow.

CHIN-LUNG:

Angrily.

Ah! One moment! Since the scholar, Wang, had spent so much money in your house, why did you drive him out into the cold?

SU SAN:

Startled.

It was not I who turned him out–it was my mistress.

CHIN-LUNG:

What a miserable woman!

P'AN:

What a brutal heart!

LIU:

But it served him right!

Chin-lung *smiles coldly, while* P'an *and* Liu *laugh heartily.*

CHIN-LUNG, P'AN, and LIU:

Proceed!

SU SAN:

In a rage, the scholar dashed out of the house and found refuge in the Temple of Duke Kuan.[4]

LIU:

How did you know that he found refuge in the Temple of Duke Kuan?

SU SAN:

One day, Chin Ko, the flower vender, whom the young scholar used to patronize in his good days, brought me word about the whereabouts of Wang. Immediately, I wrapped up some silver and went to meet my lover.

P'AN:

Did you see each other then?

SU SAN:

As soon as I saw him, disregarding the filthiness of his rags, I threw myself into his arms and wept. Then, under the altar of Duke Kuan we made love and murmured sweet words about the romance we had shared.

P'AN:

Seeing Chin-lung *deep in thought*--

Ahem! Your Honor! When I picture the meeting of the lovers under the altar, I can't help thinking of a metaphor.

CHIN-LUNG and LIU:

Which one?

P'AN:

"Playing the guitar under the huang-lien[5] tree."

CHIN-LUNG:

What do you mean by that?

P'AN:

It means seeking pleasure even in suffering.

---

4. Duke Kuan is sometimes referred to as the Chinese god of war. He had many temples all over China.
5. A plant with a bitter taste used for Chinese medicine.

LIU:

Your Honor?

CHIN-LUNG:

Yes?

LIU:

I also have a metaphor for the two lovers.

CHIN-LUNG:

What is it?

HU:

"Picking a peony even on the guillotine."

CHIN-LUNG:

What is the meaning of this metaphor?

LIU:

It means being desirous of a beautiful sweetheart even in face of death!

P'an and Liu *notice the uneasiness of* Chin-lung *and laugh together.*

CHIN-LUNG:

Uh . . . er . .

CHIN-LUNG, P'AN, and LIU:

Proceed!

SU SAN:

I persuaded him to go to Nanking[6] to compete in the government examination, but on the way he met bandits who robbed him of every single cent.

P'AN:

Ah, poor scholar! Woe was he who was robbed of everything on his way to Nanking! Oh, how tragic!

---

6. The capital in the Ming dynasty.

CHIN-LUNG:

Aye, it was really tragic, indeed!

LIU:

How can you consider it tragic? It served him right—that frequenter of brothels!

Chin-lung, P'an *and* Liu *all laugh.*

CHIN-LUNG, P'AN, and LIU:

Proceed!

SU SAN:

So all he could do was to beg in the streets.

P'AN:

Your Honor?

CHIN-LUNG:

Yes?

P'AN:

When I think of that Wang begging in the streets, it reminds me of a certain man of ancient times!

CHIN-LUNG:

Of whom?

P'AN:

A long time ago there was a nobleman's son, named Cheng Yuan-ho, who also had to beg in the streets, but later passed the government advanced examination to become a Chuang Yuan.[7] Wang may be compared to that Cheng Yuan-ho.

CHIN-LUNG:

A wonderful resemblance! Excellent!

---

7. The highest title given to the one who came out first in the government advanced examination.

LIU:

Huh! Cheng Yuan-ho was a respectable old man. How could he resemble an irresponsible spendthrift like Wang?

CHIN-LUNG:

Wang is just as good a man as Cheng; I say they do resemble each other!

P'AN:

If Your Honor says so, it must be so.

LIU:

If Your Honor says they resemble each other . . . all right! They are similar! Similar cases!

P'AN and LIU:

Ha . . . Ha . Ha!

CHIN-LUNG, P'AN, and LIU:

Proceed!

SU SAN:

Every evening, he went to the Board of Civil Offices to be their night watchman.

P'AN:

Ah! Poor nobleman Wang! He had to beg in the streets all day and spent his nights as watchman for the Board of Civil Offices. It is really pathetic!

CHIN-LUNG:

Oh . . . really pathetic, indeed!

LIU:

So Wang became the night watchman for the Board of Civil Offices! That was a downright disgrace to his ancestors!

The three judges laugh.

CHIN-LUNG, P'AN, and LIU:

Proceed!

Kneeling, Su San confesses everything to the judges, one, P'an Ping-yi, is is here seen listening attentively.

SU SAN:

The nobleman came to the house a second time to make off with some silver in order to go to Nanking.

CHIN-LUNG:

Outrageous! Since Nobleman Wang had spent thirty-six thousand ounces of silver in your house, why do you use the expression "make off with?" Didn't he have a right to get back some of his silver?

SU SAN:

Oh, I didn't mean he made away with some silver. It was I who gave it to him willingly.

CHIN-LUNG:

How much did you give him?

SU SAN:

It was very dark at night–so dark I couldn't see–and besides, there was no scale to measure it. But judging by the heft, it was not much more than three hundred ounces.

CHIN-LUNG:

Forgetting himself–

Ai-ya! Stop! On that day when I returned to the inn, I borrowed a scale to measure the silver given me. It was actually much more than three hundred ounces. Ai-ya, my dear one!

P'AN and LIU:

Ah . . . Your Honor, the imperial laws are very strict. You'd better allow her to do the confessing.

CHIN-LUNG:

Ai! Alas! I've had another stroke of the old sickness! Please pardon me and proceed with the questioning without me.

P'AN and LIU:

We'll humbly do it for you.

Wang Chin-lung *supports his head with his right hand.* P'an *and* Liu *descend from the table to the front stage and sit down on chairs placed on either side by the propman.*

P'AN:

Ah, Su San! You must confess everything according to the petition so that the Honorable High Judge will pardon you; or else you can see for yourself that he will have a stroke again!

SU SAN:

After my Scholar Wang left for Nanking, I hid myself in the northern building and pretended to be sick; for I vowed that I would never marry anyone except my beloved Wang.

LIU:

Since you had vowed that you would not marry anyone, why did you marry that Shansi merchant, Shen Yen-lin? Speak!

SU SAN:

One day as I was combing my hair in my boudoir, I heard Shen Yen-lin bragging about his wealth, saying that he was ten times as wealthy as my darling Wang. I could not stand his bragging, and I cursed him so loudly that he became embarrassed and furious. With shame and humiliation, he returned with his servant to his shop and plotted out a dirty scheme.

P'AN and LIU:

What was it?

SU SAN:

He gave a matchmaker three hundred ounces of silver and offered to that damned procuress a peck of gold. As soon as that greedy woman saw the gold, she at once sold me to Shen Yen-lin. She told me to go to the temple and thank the gods for helping my darling Wang pass the government advanced examination with the highest honors. I went to the Temple of Duke Kuan to burn incense, but to my horrible surprise, I was kidnapped, and driven to the house of Shen Yen-lin in Hung Tung.

P'AN:

How long did you stay at Hung Tung? How did Mistress P'i, Shen's wife, treat you?

SU SAN:

When I had stayed at Hung Tung for just a year, Mistress P'i planted the seed of murder. She presented me with a bowl of poisoned noodles. But, not knowing that it was poisoned, I gave it to the master, Shen Yen-lin. Not realizing the murderous plot for me, he ate it. After he had the first mouthful, he let out a blood-curdling scream, and fell down on the floor unconscious, with blood running down from the seven openings of his face. And then he was dead.

LIU:

Now–with a murder having been committed–how could Mistress P'i be willing to end her dispute with you?

SU SAN:

That was just it. Mistress P'i flew into a rage, and at once accused me of murder. She yelled to all her neighbors and the town that I was the murderess. Finally, I was dragged to the court for trial.

P'AN and LIU:

How was the trial?

SU SAN:

The first trial was fair and just.

P'AN:

How about the second one?

SU SAN:

It was different in the second trial. Everything was wrong, and I was accused as a murderess!

LIU:

How much bribe did the government in Hung Tung County receive?

SU SAN:

As far as I know, they received at least a thousand ounces of silver.

P'AND and LIU:

How much did the magistrate get?

SU SAN:

He got around eight hundred.

LIU:

Did they torture you?

SU SAN:

At first I had forty beatings and later they broke ten whips in the process of flogging me.

P'AN:

You should never have confessed to the alleged crime, no matter how hard they beat you!

SU SAN:

I didn't want to confess at first, but I simply couldn't bear those sharp, sharp blows left and right on my body. Oh. . . Oh . . . I had to yield.

Cries.

LIU:

How long have you been in prison?

SU SAN:

I have been in prison for exactly a year.

P'AN:

Have you had any visitors to see you?

SU SAN:

No, I have never had a single one.

P'AN:

What about that cursed procuress? Did she come to see you in prison?

SU SAN:

No, she did not, and she will never come to see me now.

LIU:

How about your bosom friends? Haven't they ever been to see you?

SU SAN:

Ah, my bosom friends! I lost all my bosom friends while I was in prison.

P'AN and LIU:

How about Nobleman Wang? Hasn't he been to see you in prison?

SU SAN:

Oh, Wang and I belong to two different worlds. I was but a sing-song girl – a toy to him! How can I ever expect him to remember me!

Cries.

P'AN:

If you were to see Wang now, do you think you could still recognize him?

SU SAN:

Of course, I can. Even though he may be a high official with a grand title and a fancy hat, I shall always recognize him.

P'AN:

He may be a high official now, but if he does not choose to remember you, it's useless.

SU SAN:

If my lover comes to me . .

P'AN and LIU:

Then what?

SU SAN:

I am willing to die and will be contented in the next world.

P'an *and* Liu *stand up and go downstage right.*

LIU:

To P'an:

Ah! Your Honor! What shall we do? In questioning the prisoner, we have involved our senior . . .

Making a sign at Wang Chin-lung–

very deeply in the case. Let's leave the courtroom for the moment and see what he will do about all this mess.

P'AN ans LIU:

To Wang Chin-lung–

Your Honor, may we be excused from court?

CHIN-LUNG:

Raising his head–

You may be excused!

P'an *and* Liu *leave together to the left. Four court scribes and four guards enter from either side.*

CHIN-LUNG:

To himself. Aside.

Su San! My dear Su San! How I long to come from this high seat and take you in my arms, but . ahem . . .

Gazing at the stern guards–

The imperial law is very strict. I can only lower my head and think .

Wang Chin-lung *gestures to call to* Su San, *but hesitates. Then–*

I have an idea! I'll order Judge Liu Ping-yi to take over the case.

Turns toward guards–

Guard!

A GUARD:

Yes, Your Honor?

CHIN-LUNG:

Present this card of mine to Judge Liu and tell him I wish to see him.

GUARD:

Yes, Your Honor.

Exits to the left.

CHIN-LUNG:

Su San, you may leave, for the moment. I assure you this court will do its utmost to save you from the death penalty.

SU SAN:

Thank you, Your Honor.

Su San *rises and rubs her tired knees. Aside.*

It was fortunate for me not to have suffered from any torture in this trial. I am relieved, at last. Leaving this courtroom, let me turn my head and take a look at the High Judge . .

Su San *turns her head to look at* Chin-lung, *but the guards prevent her from doing so.*

The imperial laws are strict, indeed. Let me say some sweet words of yore and see if he will be touched.

To Chin-lung:

Su San is like the nectar of a flower, in the spring.

CHIN-LUNG:

What about her lover, Wang?

SU SAN:

Ah, Your Honor! . . her lover, Wang, is like a humming bird, flying to and fro, gathering honey from the heart of the flower in its blossoming time. But now, Scholar Wang is seen no more. Ah, San Lang . . .

Su San *attempts to fly into* Chin-lung's *arms, but he–not desiring to let the guards know–waves his sleeve to stop her.*

Ah . . . Alas . . Where is the humming bee when the flower is faded and and withered . . ah!

CHIN-LUNG:

No more talk! You'd better leave the court!

SU SAN:

Yes, Your Honor!

Starts to walk toward the imaginary door downstage center.

Very sorrowfully I leave the court.

Raises one foot to pass the imaginary threshold and walks to downstage right.

I will wait and see how he settles my case.

Exit Su San *upstage right. Enter four servants in black gowns with white collars and undersleeves, followed by* Judge Liu *from the left.*

LIU:

Salutations to Your Honor! May I inquire of Your Honor's purpose in summoning me?

CHIN-LUNG:

I have transferred the case of Su San into Your Honor's hands, you must bear the circumstances in mind!

LIU:

I will judge strictly in accordance with the law–no more and no less!

CHIN-LUNG:

My trust is in you to do so. But conceal as much as you can.

Exit four court scribes, guards, and Wang Chin-lung *to the left.*

LIU:

Aside.

Hah! I know you are involved in this case, and yet you ordered me to "bear the circumstances in mind!" Phew! Wang Chin-lung! Ah, Wang Chin-lung! If you have nothing to do with the murder itself, it will be well; but if you are involved–you will be ruined! Ha, ha, Your future is in my hands! I, Liu Ping-yi, am an official to serve the emperor . . . why should I be the running dog of Wang Chin-lung? Since he is now in my hands, I'll play a trick or two on him.

The four servants and Liu *go off to the left.*

SCENE THREE

The women's prison where Su San *is confined.*

Downstage center is a chair placed sideways, with its back facing the audience to denote the prison gates.

In the center of the stage is a table with two chairs on either side.

Enter Wang Chin-lung *from upstage right. He is now disguised as a scholar, a black gown, white collar, white undersleeves, and a black hat.*

CHIN-LUNG:

I saw Su San during the trial in court, but what was the use if I could not openly recognize her? Ah! If Yü T'ang Ch'un had not given me money to go to Nanking to compete in the government advanced examination, this would never have happened! I must try my utmost to save her. I can't bear to see my lover suffer in prison! I have disguised myself as a scholar to see and comfort her.

Approaches the chair downstage center.

Ah, here I am, right in front of the women's prison. Hey, open the door!

Enter the Warden *from the right. She is a stern, middle-aged woman dressed in a dark blue jacket and trousers, carrying a set of keys.*

WARDEN:

Aside.

I like money—you like money—who says he doesn't like money is a fake! By the order of Judge Liu, I am to ask for money—as much as I like—from the one who comes to see Su San! Ha! Ha! What a lucky day for me! I hear someone at the prison gates. I hope he wants to see Su San! Hey, coming,

coming!

Comes near the chair downstage center and stands behind the chair. .

Are you a prisoner?

CHIN-LUNG:

No, but I want to see a prisoner.

WARDEN:

Here!

Stretches out her hand for silver.

CHIN-LUNG:

What do you mean?

WARDEN:

Silver coins!

Chin-lung *takes out imaginary silver coins and gives them to the* Warden, *who puts them in her pocket and moves the chair aside for him to enter.*

All right, come in.

Chin-lung *lowers his head and lifts his foot to denote that he enters the prison gates, then the* Warden *replaces the chair as before.*

Now, whom do you want to see, young man?

CHIN-LUNG:

I want to see Su San!

WARDEN:

Showing excitement and pleasure.

Ah, you want to see Su San, eh!

Aside.

Oh dear, heaven has sent me wealth!

To Wang Chin-lung:

Some more!

Stretches out her hand again.

CHIN-LUNG:

What?

WARDEN:

Silver!

CHIN-LUNG:

But I have already given you silver!

WARDEN:

Price depends upon the quality of the commodities! The more valuable the commodity, the higher the price!

CHIN-LUNG:

All right, all right!

He yields, and again gives her a few silver coins.

WARDEN:

Pleased, she puts the silver coins in her pocket.

You wait here and let me call Su San out for you.

Turning to upstage right–

Su San! There is someone here to see you!

Enter Su San *from the right.*

SU SAN:

Oh, woe is me! Ai-ya! Someone to see me? Ai, I can't believe my ears . . . Mother Warden, who is it?

WARDEN:

I don't know!

SU SAN:

Where is he?

WARDEN:

Follow me.

Su San *follows the* Warden *downstage.*

Here he is.

Chin-lung and Su San fly into each other's arms and weep.

CHIN-LUNG:

Ai-ya! My Su San!

SU SAN:

Ai-ya! My San Lang! I can't help weeping when I see my lover here with me, so near and yet so far.

SU SAN and CHIN-LUNG:

Ah, my beloved! Ah, my dearest!

Su San gazes bashfully at the Warden, but the Warden—pretending not to understand—does not move a step.

CHIN-LUNG:

Hey! Mother Warden! Go away!

WARDEN:

What?

CHIN-LUNG:

Go away! Get out!

WARDEN:

Go away, eh? Some more, then!

Stretches out her hand.

CHIN-LUNG:

What? What do you want?

WARDEN:

Laughing—

Still some more silver!

CHIN-LUNG:

Ai-ya-ya! How greedy you are!

Chin-lung gives a piece of silver to the Warden and pushes her toward the left.

WARDEN:

You'd better be quick in whatever you want to say to her.

Exit Warden to the left.

Chin-lung sits on the left and Su San on the right, in the center of the stage.

SU SAN:

Hai!

Sighs.

Ah, San Lang! I have suffered so much for you; why did you not recognize me in the courtroom this morning? Is it because you want to forget our sweet days of love for each other?

CHIN-LUNG:

Ah, dear San! In the courtroom during the trial, it was not because I didn't want to recognize you. I just couldn't do it because of the strict imperial law. Therefore, I have come here tonight to apologize for not having recognized you openly in the court and to talk about old times.

SU SAN:

Weeps and sighs.

Hai! You! You are a nobleman! A high official now! I am but a prisoner, suffering and pining away my hours and days in jail. Now that you are an officer of the highest rank in the imperial government, you wanted to show off your power and dignity during the trial in the courtroom. Woe is me to have given silver and my love to the wrong, ungrateful man! Ou . . . O . . . !

Cries.

CHIN-LUNG:

Very sad and uneasy, goes over to Su San.

Su San, my dear San! Please cry no more, dear.
You know I am not that kind of man!

Wipes away her tears and caresses her.

Let's not think of the past. It is gone.

SU SAN:

Oh, San Lang, you must quickly think of a way to save me!

CHIN-LUNG:

Through the kindness of His Imperial Majesty, I was made Chuang Yuan and thereupon appointed to inspect the criminal cases of eight counties. The Shansi provincial judge, Liu Ping-yi, is my subordinate and I have just tried to ask him to judge you favorably. But he–being a good and fair judge–only said, "I will judge according to law." Now, I have determined to save you and get you out of jail at the risk of losing my high position. Please do be a little patient, darling. I assure you I will try my very best to save you.

SU SAN:

I hope you can!

Enter the Warden *from the left.*

WARDEN:

Very excitedly–

Ai-ya! Oh! What shall I do? Oh!

CHIN-LUNG:

Mother Warden, what's the matter?

WARDEN:

Judge Liu is coming! Now he is going to inspect the prison and you are here! Ai-ya, what shall I do?

CHIN-LUNG:

To himself:

Heavens! Judge Liu is my subordinate. If I let him see me here, it will be terrible What shall I do?

Gestures to think by putting his two fingers on his right temple.

I've got it; let me pretend to be insane and rush out of jail!

Chin-lung *turns his back to the audience and paints his face with a few black strokes. He turns around, lifts his right sleeve, and gestures to get out of the prison gate downstage center. At this moment,* Judge Liu, *carrying a lantern,*[8] *enters the stage from upstage right, while the* Warden *leads* Su San *off to the left exit at the rear of the stage.* Chin-lung *feigns madness and collides with* Judge Liu, *who falls down with the lantern while* Chin-lung *dashes from the stage.* Judge Liu *gets up and holds the lantern high in order to catch sight of the man who has made him fall—but too late.*

LIU:

I wanted to play a trick on others, and yet I was played a fool instead. Let the lantern lead the way to my residence.

Exit Liu *to the right.*

SCENE FOUR

The courtroom as in Scene Two.

There are four guards with swords and spears, four court scribes, and four court officers standing in two's on either side. As in the other scene, Chin-lung *is seated in the center, with* Judge P'an *on the right and* Judge Liu *on the left.*

CHIN-LUNG:

Bring in the criminals for trial!

Two guards go off to the right and bring in Chao Chien-sheng, Mistress P'i *and* Ch'un Chin. Chao Chien-sheng, Mistress P'i's *paramour, is a shrewd and treacherous man of 40, dressed in a green-silk gown.* Mistress P'i, Shen Yen-lin's *widow, is a crafty woman of 35. She is dressed in white, the color of mourning in China. Her appearance is not unpleasant but not amiable enough to attract one to come near her and trust her in any way.* Ch'un Chin *is the servant girl, sprightly, clever, and active. She seems to be full of gossip. She is dressed in a pink blouse and bright-blue trousers.* Chien-sheng *and* P'i *kneel side by side, with* Ch'un Chin behind them.

8. The lantern, to indicate night on the Capital Opera stage, is always unlighted to secure safety in the theater; it is used as a dancing aid in accordance with the symbolic action so common in Chinese stage convention.

CHIEN-SHENG' P'I, and CU'UN CHIN:

We kneel and kowtow before Your Honors!

CHIN-LUNG:

How did you murder Shen Yen-lin? Confess immediately!

MISTRESS P'I:

I made two bowls of noodles with mutton. I ate a bowl and I am still all right and alive; but my husband ate the other bowl and died. Su San must have put some poison in my hustands's bowl. I beseech Your Honors to right this grievance.

CHIN-LUNG:

Who brought the noodles to Shen Yen-lin?

CH'UN CHIN:

Very quickly and flirtatiously–

I did. Madam ordered me to take the bowl of noodles to the master's room.

CHIN-LUNG:

You must be the one who put the poison in the noodles.

CH'UN CHIN:

Good Lord! Heavens! No. I am not the one who killed the master. My dear honorable judges, if you want to find out who is our master's murderer, you'd better ask this Chien-sheng. He'll tell you.

CHIN-LUNG:

Chao Chien-sheng! Since you are a scholar, your place should be in the study. Why are you mixed up in other people's business?

CHIEN-SHENG:

I have been a devoted scholar since the age of five. Shen Yen-lin and I were great friends. Since I am an honest man, he used to ask me to take care of his family whenever he was off on business. But since Shen Yen-lin took Su San home as his concubine, there was no peace in their home–quarreling and bickering–morning and night. Although Su San was marrred to Shen, she hardly had a chance to see him.

Looks at Mistress P'i–

Besides, Mistress P'i made Su San do manual labor–carrying pails of water from the well to the kitchen and washing clothes. One day Su San became sick and, in her delirium, she uttered her inner desire to murder Shen Yen-lin so that she could fly to her lover . . .

CHIN-LUNG

How do you know she has a lover?

CHIEN-SHENG:

Once I saw her–with my own eyes–standing there dreamily and longingly under a big tree and I heard her–with my own ears–murmuring,

Imitating a girl's voice–

"San Lang, San Lang!" If it isn't her lover's name that she was calling, whose is it? Since she has a lover, she must have been the one who murdered Shen Yen-lin! I beseech you to see the facts and the logic of it all!

CHIN-LUNG:

Bah! You and your lies! I can see you will not confess without torture! Come, guards! Torture him!

Two guards approach Chien-sheng.

CHIEN-SHENG:

Excitedly–

Oh, please don't! Don't! I'll confess! I'll confess!

CHIN-LUNG:

All right, guards. Let him confess.

The guards resume their places.

CHIEN-SHENG:

It was Mistress P'i who murdered Shen Yen-lin. Since I have always been P'i's paramour, it was I who bought the poison from a druggist! P'i's intention was to poison Su San. Who would have thought Shen Yen-lin would swallow the poisoned noodles? You see, that caused his sudden death!

CHIN-LUNG:

Is all that true?

CHIEN-SHENG:

The whole truth and nothing but the truth!

CHIN-LUNG:

Come, scribes, make him sign his confession!

A scribe holds out paper and brush for him to sign.

Mistress P'i! You wanted to murder Su San with the poisoned noodles, but unexpectedly they were eaten by Shen Yen-lin, who was killed instantly. Such a cruel and villainous woman deserves the penalty of execution without hesitation. Now, are you going to confess to your crime or not?

P'I:

Very flirtatiously–

Ah, Your Honor, don't be angry with me! I will confess!

To Chien-sheng:

If I must die, let's die together! Let me sign my confession too!

Another secretary holds out paper and brush for her to sign the confession.

P'i *and* Chien-sheng *get up and stand on the right.*

CH'UN CHIN:

Oh, Your Honor! These two are the murderers. I am only a slave, bought to serve my mistress. I have had nothing to do with the murder. Besides, I have an old mother who has to depend on me! Oh, my dear judges, please do have mercy on me and let me go!

CHIN-LUNG:

Ha! You three conspired to do a wicked deed–one is just as villainous and crafty as the other! How can the court let you go free? Come, make her sign the confession!

Another secretary takes the notebook to her and she signs, then stands to the left.

CHIN-LUNG:

To the guards:

Bring in Su San!

A guard goes, faces upstage right, and yells, "Bring in Su San."
The Warden *brings in* Su San *from the right.*
Su San *kneels before the judges and the* Warden *exits to the right.*

CHIN-LUNG:

Su San! This court has righted your grievance. Shen Yen-lin was murdered by Mistress P'i and her paramour, Chao Chien-sheng, and that corrupt magistrate of Hung Tung was bribed to make you confess to the alleged crime. Now I will summon Magistrate Wang to confess before this court.

SU SAN:

Thank you, Your Honor!

She rises and stands to the left.

CHIN-LUNG:

Come, guards! Summon the Magistrate of Hung Tung County.

The guard calls and Magistrate Wang *enters from the right. He bows, kneels, and kowtows before the judges.*

CHIN-LUNG:

Magistrate, how much did you get from Su San's husband murder case?

MAGISTRATE WANG:

I didn't get any bribe from that case at all. Su San willingly confessed to the crime. I don't accept bribes!

CHIN-LUNG:

Rubbish! You said you didn't accept bribes! Here's the signed confession of Chao Chien-sheng. Take a look at it yourself!

A secretary hands him the paper and he reads it.

CHIN-LUNG:

Now, do you still dare to deny the truth?

MAGISTRATE WANG:

Oh, but Chien-sheng *gave* me the silver—I didn't ask for it!

JUDGE LIU:

Ah, Magistrate! Since you received a thousand ounces of silver, how much did each of your court officers get for his share?

MAGISTRATE WANG:

They are all very honest, so they didn't accept a cent.

CHIEN-SHENG:

Hai!

Sighs.

Magistrate! Don't you remember the eight hundred ounces of silver I gave you on the second day?

JUDGE LIU:

Now that your witness is right here before you, can you deny anything? You'd better confess.

MAGISTRATE WANG:

Oh, Your Honor! This is the first time that I have ever accepted bribes. I will never do it again. So, Your Honors, please do have mercy on me!

CHIN-LUNG:

Ai! You are supposed to treat the people like your own children and right their grievances, and yet you accepted bribes and acted against heaven. If I do not punish you severely, how can I face the emperor! Come!

To the guards:

Take off his official hat!

A guard takes off the Magistrate's *hat.*

Su San, come and bear witness against him!

SU SAN:

Yes, Your Honor!

She steps up and points at the Magistrate.

Corrupt official, you! In the first trial you were kind to me, not treating me like a murderess. But you changed your attitude after you received the bribe, and had me beaten hundreds of times. You almost put an end to my life. I was fortunate to be tried by these honorable judges, who have found out the truth, righted the wrong done to me, and saved me from execution. If you call yourself an official with a parental love for the people, how can you do such a shameful thing? Now that everything is clear, do you regret your sin or not?

MAGISTRATE WANG:

All right, enough, enough! Please don't rub it in. This is what I get for accepting bribes.

CHIN-LUNG:

Remorse doesn't help. The court is being especially kind to you. You are to be dismissed from your post. You may go back to your home town when the new magistrate takes over your office.

MAGISTRATE WANG:

Thank you, my dear honorable judge! Many thanks to both of you, too, Your Honors!

He kowtows before Chin-lung, Liu, *and* P'an

LIU and P'AN:

To the Magistrate:

Get out!

Magistrate Wang *gets up and exits to the left.*

CHIN-LUNG:

Ah, Su San!

Su San *kneels down.*

You suffered a gross grievance. You were lucky that we came in time to save you from execution! Now, because you have suffered much for a year in prison, I'm going to compensate you. I shall reward you with a red cape and some golden flowers for your hair. For three days you shall parade in the streets of the city in a sedan chair to show all the people that you are innocent. After that, you may live in the Temple of the Goddess of Mercy.

SU SAN:

Thank you, most merciful, honorable judge.

Su San receives a red cape, and golden flowers are placed in her hair by the guards. She gets up. Seeing Mistress P'i–

P'i! You shameless woman! I didn't want to marry Shen Yen-lin, but it was he who tricked me by saying he would find my lover for me. You did me a great favor when you prevented me from seeing Shen Yen-lin. It was a blessing in disguise, indeed! I never imagined you had an affair with Chien-sheng and plotted with him to kill me. And I never expected Shen Yen-lin would unwittingly eat up the poisoned noodles and die for me. You even accused me of murder. Now look at me! Look at my red cape and golden flowers! How glorious and honored am I! I hope you have learned that "You ruin only yourself when you try to ruin others."

CHIN-LUNG:

Come, guards, prepare the sedan chair and a big cymbal for Su San to parade all over the city for three days, and then send her to the Temple of the Goddess of Mercy. As for the criminals, have them removed and put in chains.

P'i, Chien-sheng, Ch'un Chin, *and guards all exit to the left.*

SU SAN:

Rises.

Thank you, Your Honor! With joy and dignity, I ll walk out of the courtroom to parade in grand style for three days, and then to the Temple.

Exits to the left.

CHIN-LUNG:

Your Honors!

LIU and P'AN:

Yes, Your Honor?

CHIN-LUNG:

What do you think of my judgment on the case of Su San?

LIU:

Excellent judgment, Your Honor! But how are you going to punish the criminals?

CHIN-LUNG:

Let us think of a special punishment for each of the three criminals.

LIU:

Mistress P'i?

CHIN-LUNG:

She murdered her own husband in cold blood, so according to law, she should be strangled to death.

LIU:

Her original purpose was to kill Su San, but she murdered Shen Yen-lin instead; so wouldn't a simple execution of beheading be adequate punishment for her?

CHIN-LUNG:

All right, execution by simple beheading for her, then! How about Chien-sheng?

LIU:

He secretly bought the poison, committed adultery, and bribed the officials and guards. He is an enemy of the people, and thus he deserves the severe punishment of execution by beheading and having his head hung up in the market place as a warning against sinning.

P'AN:

Good! Good for him! It serves him right! Your Honors: what about that slave girl, Ch'un Chin? What crime shall we punish her for?

CHIN-LUNG:

Nothing in the world can be achieved without an agent or a go-between. The murder of Shen Yen-lin and the adultery of P'i were both committed through the help of Ch'un Chin. She is a ringleader, as far as crime is concerned.

LIU:

So execute her without fail, that's all!

P'AN:

Just a moment! Ch'un Chin is but a young slave girl who is supposed to obey orders! What could she do to violate the orders of her mistress? Your Honors, I beseech you to consider her difficult situation!

CHIN-LUNG:

Are you pleading for her?

P'AN:

Yes, Your Honor, have mercy!

LIU:

Then, let us make the decision in court. We trust our judgment will be sound and just.

Pause.

Now, when I think of it, putting Su San in a nunnery at the Temple of the Goddess of Mercy is not a long-range and wise plan. May I ask you, Your Honor–if you will excuse my impertinence–whether Your Honor is married or not?

CHIN-LUNG:

Embarrassed;

Ah, that . . . No, I haven't got a wife yet!

LIU:

Judge P'an and my humble self would like to be matchmakers for your Honor and Su San to be bound in wedlock. I wonder what Your Honor's opinion is.

CHIN-LUNG:

More embarrassed but well pleased.

Well . uh . . . .

P'AN:

No more talk, Judge Liu. Let's get to work. Come, guards! Bring in the criminals!

Two guards respond with "Aye, exit to the left, and return with P'i, Chien-sheng, *and* Ch'un Chin, *who kneel before the judges.*

LIU:

Now, with this precious sword of the Grand Judge, execute Chao Chien-sheng and Mistress P'i. Then take Ch'un Chin to the women's jail, where she will live the rest of her life.

Chien-sheng, P'i *and* Ch'un Chin *start to go, toward the left.*

CHIEN-SHENG:

This is what I get for trying to harm others The old saying "In trying to ruin others, one ruins only oneself" is true indeed.

Sighs.

P'I:

Cheer up, my dear. At least we can be husband and wife in the underworld.

Chien-sheng, P'i, *and* Ch'un Chin *all exit to upstage left.*

CHIN-LUNG:

Thank you for being matchmakers for me, Your Honors. I thank you!

Bows with clasped hands.

LIU and P'AN:

Three days later we shall come to Your Honor's wedding feast.

CHIN-LUNG:

Of course, I shall invite you both!

LIU and P'AN;

May we be excused!

Chin-lung *exits to the left, followed by all.*

(CURTAIN)

TWO MEN ON A STRING

(Feng Yi Ting)

Two Men on a String is one of the most famous historical plays of China, based on a story concerning the last days of the great Han dynasty, just before the Chinese empire was broken apart into The Three Kingdoms (*circa* 220 A D.). The plot is woven around Tiao Ch'an, who is not only beautiful and charming, but clever enough to bring about the downfall of Tung Cho, a traitorous prime minister of the Han who had the ambition to become emperor himself. During the course of the play, Tiao Ch'an also manages to snare a handsome mate, the famed warrior, Lü Pu.

Although Tiao Ch'an is a fictitious character, history records that there was a love affair between the concubine of Tung Cho and the warrior, Lü Pu. There is also some evidence of a plot to use the talents of the concubine to destroy Tung Cho.

The Chinese name of this Capital Opera play, *Feng Yi T'ing* (鳳儀亭), can be translated as simply "Phoenix Pavilion." This garden pavilion is the scene of the crucial action of the play. In English, *Two Men on a String* seems a more apt, descriptive title, and so is used.

The play somewhat resembles Corneille's *Le Cid* and other heroic plays of the

French classical period, with their themes of honor, love, and patriotism, and the characters totally good or totally evil.

As in the other four plays in this book, the art does not lie in the plot, the language, or the theme. The reader must realize that this is an English translation of the bare skeleton of the opera on which are hung the artistic pearls of song, dance, costume, and–above all–acting full of symbolic gestures known and understood by the audience. A Western playwright would find it difficult to encompass this story in one play because his audience demands logical transitions between changes in motivation of characters–or consistency in such motivation. In the Chinese play it is almost as though long scenes in which the psychology of an individual character is examined and shifts in motives explained have been excised. The audience is quite willing to accept this as being understood and would rather not be bored with watching the process. Because of this condensation, you have horrendous murders, lies, and inhuman actions seemingly accepted as a matter of course by the other characters in the play; the audience uses its imagination to make these abrupt transitions ring true.

This play was performed in Chinese by the Foo Hsing School of Dramatic Art that fascinated every spectator as they toured the United States, Canada, Central and South Americas in 1963-64. It was a Hurok production and was re-entitled *The Beautiful Bait* in English. Some parts were filmed by the Chinese Government Information Service in Taiwan and it may be rented free by writing to the Office of Press Counselor Chinese Embassy in Washington, D. C.

TWO MEN ON A STRING
Characters

TIAO CH'AN . . . . *the beauty*
(董 卓)

WANG YUN . . . . *minister of Education*
(王 允)

TUNG CHO . . . . *Prime Minister*
(貂 嬋)

LU PU . . . . *brave young adopted son of Tung Cho*
(呂 布)

CHANG WEN . . . . *high military official*
(張 温)

LI SU . . . . *military official*
(李 肅)

SERVANTS

GUARDS

SLAVE GIRLS

SCENE ONE

The stage represents a spacious room without much decoration, except a low, rectangular table and three large yellow cushions, for which ordinary tables and chairs with red satin draperies are used. In the background the audience envisions a veranda overlooking the courtyard.

The table is now placed on center stage with two chairs on either side.

Enter Wang Yün, *a scholarly man of sixty-five, medium build, quiet and worried, wearing the typical civic official robe, from upstage right.*

Chang Wen, *a stout man of forty-five in the conventional military attire, also enters, from upstage right.*

WANG YUN:

Rebellious minister! Thieving son! Worthy of this era!

CHANG WEN:

Such a one should be eradicated . . . Please sit down, Your Excellency.

WANG YUN:

All right . . . Hai . .

Sighs, seats himself on left and Chang on right.

CHANG WEN:

Why do you sigh so, Your Excellency?

WANG:

Only because of a traitor in our court, whose outrageous actions become more reckless each day. It will lead inevitably to rebellion and usurpation of the throne.

CHANG:

It could only be that Tung . . .

WANG:

Sh . . . sh! Be careful! Not so loud!

Standing up, looking around and listening cautiously to both sides–

Yes, exactly! It's that old bandit, Tung Cho!

CHANG:

You don't have to worry any more, Your Excellency. I have written secretly to Yuan Shu, asking him to arrange with the nobles to despatch troops to surround the capital. When that is accomplished, you and I can secretly notify the civil and military officials within. With cooperation from both within and without the capital, how can this traitor escape?

WANG:

All this has to be done in secret, or both our families would certainly be destroyed!

A VOICE:

Off stage.

The Prime Minister, Tung Cho.

Music–big gong, cymbals, small gong, cymbals . . .

WANG and CHANG:

Get up and walk to downstage center.

Together, and bowing with clasped hands–

Salutations!

From upstage right, enter Tung Cho, *a stout, robust man, about sixty, with a white painted face* and *a gray, full-beard. He is followed by four attendants.*

WANG YUN:

Greetings, Your Excellency!

TUNG CHO:

I see both of you are already here.

WANG:

We have waited some time for Your Excellency; I wonder why we are summoned here.

TUNG CHO:

Gentlemen, in front of the Tiger Pen Pass the armies of the eighteen great nobles were defeated, and they have already retreated. This is wonderful news for the Emperor!

WANG:

Your Excellency is as awe-inspiring as a tiger!

TUNG CHO:

I have ordered wine and food for us here in the Chancery to celebrate our victory.

Gestures Chang *and* Wang *to sit down.*

CHANG and WANG:

We thank you, Your Excellency.

They all sit, before the three separate tables, as set by the propman and the attendants pour imaginary wine into the cups.

TUNG CHO:

Facing the audience, with Chang *on his right and* Wang *on his left–*

To your health, gentlemen!

Raising his cup as Lü Pu, *a young, handsome warrior, excitedly enters from the left of the audience.*

LU PU:

There is some secret business I must tell you, my father.

TUNG CHO:

What's all the excitement? Why do you look so angry?

LU PU:

Please leave the table for a moment; I have something vitally important to tell you.

TUNG:

What's the harm of telling me right here?

The *Ching* or the painted face: the white to denote cunningness and deception and the full beard to denote wealth and power.

LU PU:

There are too many ears and eyes here.

TUNG:

Come closer, then.

Lü Pu *comes closer and whispers into* Tung's *ear.*

LU PU:

Aloud.

There is a letter, too, my father. Please read it for yourself.

TUNG CHO:

After reading the letter–

Ah! Seize that old dog, Chang Wen, and behead him before all these people. At once!

LU PU:

Yes, Your Excellency.

Lü Pu *approaches* Chang Wen.

Chang Wen, you've secretly plotted with Yuan Shu against my father and me. Now don't you dare to move a step.

Pulling out his sword–

Here's the reward for your pains.

Thrusts the sword into Chang Wen's *neck. Chang Wen lowers his head, and slips away upstage left.*

WANG YUN:

Ai-ya, without the Emperor's order, how dare you kill a high official like General Chang? How? . . . why? . . .

TUNG CHO:

Wang Yün, what is your complaint?

WANG:

What crime has Chang Wen committed, may I ask?

TUNG:

That old rescal has conspired with Yuan Shu against us both, so I had him beheaded.

WANG:

What proof have you?

TUNG:

The letter is here. Have a look at it yourself.

Giving Wang Yün *the letter.*

WANG:

After reading the letter–

Chang Wen! Alas, Chang Wen! The Prime Minister is in the court. Loyalty should be to the empire. Since you've secretly plotted for his life, you undoubtedly deserved your death!

TUNG:

Show me the bastard's head, guards, and then let us make haste for the palace.

The guards bring in Chang Wen's *head*[1] *on a platter.* Tung Cho *looks at it with scorn and then exits to the left, followed by* Lü Pu *and attendants.*

WANG:

Alone.

Brutal usurper, you! Poor loyal one! Fate was certainly unkind that the secret was untimely ripped from you. How cruelly you met your death! There must be revenge for your heroic sacrifice for the dynasty of Han!

Exit to the left.

SCENE TWO

The stage represents the back garden in Wang Yün's *home. A new moon is supposed to be half hidden by the hanging willow tree on the left. The audience imagines flowers artistically arranged in flower beds in the back-*

1 A decapitated head on the Chinese opera stage is usually represented by a red bundle.

ground. Upstage we can envision a corner of Wang Yün s *study, with a table on which scrolls are laid.*

Next morning–2 a.m.

Enter Tiao Ch'an *alone, from upstage right, with an incense pot in her hands. She is a very beautiful girl of eighteen, quiet and full of determination. She wears a pink blouse and a long, white, flowing skirt. In her hair there are flowers and decorations. She is now singing and dancing as lightly as a fairy, yet looks worried and sad.*

TIAO CH'AN:

Dancing and singing
Under the flowers,
In the quiet and dark of night
I secretly sigh–I cannot sleep.
The moon, with the flowers
Playing hide and seek,
Glides her way to the west wall;
But I–with my endless sorrow–
Cannot rest,
As time passes silently away.

Speaks.

I, Tiao Ch'an, a slave singer in the house of Wang Yün, have been taught all the arts–singing, dancing, writing, and reading. My master has treated me like his own daughter ever since I came here as a young child. I have noticed my master growing more and more melancholy. Although he does not utter a word about it, I can see he is worried about state affairs. It's too bad there isn't someone to help him. Ah, I wish I were a man I'd give my life for him and my country.

I dare not tell him how I feel. Oh, greediness of man! What man will not do to obtain wealth and power! It makes me blush to think of it. If man could only realize the truth that money means nothing, what a happy world it would be.

Steps are heard approaching.

Here comes the master! He looks even more anxious tonight. I must not let him find me here alone . . . I'd better hide.

Tiao Ch'an *hides herself behind a tree (imaginary) on the left. Enter* Wang Yün *from the right.*

WANG:

Oh, Heaven! . . . On this moonlit night, I pray to you for help, for strength, for hope, for . . . an idea, for . . . a scheme. That cold-blooded rascal killed Chang Wen–a high official–before our very eyes at the banquet and without the Emperor's order. Oh, Goddess of the Moon! May I be given an idea to destroy that cruel traitor–to avenge my friend's heroic death! Oh, Heaven! I'm sure you know how cunning and wicked Tung Cho is! He intends to usurp the throne of Han; with the help of his adopted son, Lü Pu, he has killed everyone who dares oppose him. Oh, Heaven! Hear me! Give me an idea! Justice must be done! That traitor must be wiped out! Oh, Heaven, I, Wang Yün, with a heart of loyalty to the House of Han, am kneeling before you –in tears–to beg for assistance! I pray to heaven!

Tiao Ch'an *accidentally drops her pin.*

Oh, who is there? Come out at once!

TIAO CH'AN:

Comes out from behind the tree.

It's I, oh master.

WANG:

Surprised.

Is that you, Tiao Ch'an?

TIAO CH'AN:

Yes, master.

WANG:

Angrily.

What are you doing here at this time of night?

Suspiciously.

Are you planning to have a rendezvous with a lover?

TIAO CH'AN:

You've always treated me like your own daughter. How could I do such a disgraceful thing?

WANG:

If you don't have any rendezvous, why are you here in the back garden alone at such a late hour?

Showing his anger

TIAO CH'AN:

Please don't be angry with me, master. Let me explain!

WANG:

Go ahead! And don't hide anything from me!

TIAO CH'AN:

All right, I'll tell you. Ever since I came here, you and madame have brought me up kindly and tenderly. I am ready to give up my life for you both in return for your love and training. But I have noticed that lately you, my master, are greatly worried and anxious. Not daring to ask you, I have come here to think about it. If I can be of any service, I am willing to sacrifice my life to help you.

WANG:

Upset but pleased. Obviously suddenly struck with an idea.

Who would think that the destiny of the empire could be in your delicate hands, my girl! This is not the place to talk. Let's go into the study.

TIAO CH'AN

Yes, master.

Wang Yün, *followed by* Tiao Ch'an, *walks to downstage center and gestures to step into the study.*

WANG:

The destiny of Han is now in your hands if you can be absolutely loyal and courageous.

TIAO CH'AN:

My master, as I have said before, if there is any need for my service, I will not be afraid of a thousand deaths.

WANG:

At present, the people of the empire are on the verge of danger and are greatly agitated. Only you can save them. That traitor, Tung Cho, has nurtured the evil desire of usurpation and no one can stop him. Besides, he has an adopted son, Lü Pu, who is very brave and shrewd. Nothing can escape his fingers. All the nobles–and both military and civil officials–are afraid of him. However, I have noticed that both Tung Cho and Lü Pu have a weakness for women and wine! Therefore, I want to use a beauty trap. First, I'll have you betrothed to Lü Pu and then have you marry Tung Cho. Later, you must underhandedly stir up jealousy and hatred between these two, so that finally you induce Lü Pu to kill that heartless usurper in order to restore power to the Emperor. Tiao Ch'an, my child–you will be the greatest heroine in the Empire of Han!

TIAO CH'AN:

Just present me to Lü Pu and I will do the rest.

WANG:

Now, you must be firm and steady in your mission. If you are false and disclose the secret, our family will be completely destroyed. Since we have always looked upon you as our own child, be cautious.

TIAO CH'AN:

My dear master, if I should prove ungrateful, may I deserve the penalty of a million swords.

WANG:

I salute your loyalty!

Kowtows.

TIAO CH'AN:

Oh, my master! How can I stand such courtesy from you!

Kneels down at once.

WANG:

Gets up and sings.

If you can destroy that cold-blooded traitor
And save the country from ruin,
You will be a great heroine indeed!
And your name will live forever and ever!

TIAO CH'AN:

Sings.

Worry no more, my lord.
In getting rid of this monster,
I will do double service:
To you, who are wholeheartedly true;
And to my land, the empire of Han.

Tiao Ch'an *rises and exits to the left.*

WANG:

Alone

It is said that Lü Pu has lost his precious headdress in the battle in front of Tiger Pen Pass. I will have one made especially for him, with diamonds and emeralds from my family chest. This will lure him to my house to meet Tiao Ch'an and fall into the beauty trap. Ah, long live the House of Han!

Exit Wang Yün *to the right.*

SCENE THREE

The following afternoon.
The same setting as Scene One, but a chair is now placed in front of the table.
This is the residence of Wang Yün.
Wang *enters from upstage right, walks downstage center, turns around and goes to sit,while a servant enters quietly from upstage left and stands by.*

WANG:

I have had the beautiful headdress sent to Lü Pu, and today he will come here to thank me personally. A marvelous beginning points to a marvelous ending.

To the Servant:

Set the table and prepare wine.

SERVANT:

Yes, my lord.

WANG:

When Lü Pu is here and drinks his fill, announce that a messenger from the Western Palace wants me for a conference. Come several times to give the same report. Now, can you remember your task?

SERVANT:

Yes, my lord.

Exit the Servant *to the left.*

A VOICE:

Off stage.

General Lü Pu.

Enter Lü Pu *from upstage right.*

Wang Yün *gets up, walks downstage center, gestures to step out, walks to downstage center, bows with clasped hands.*

LU PU:

Greetings to the Minister of Education!

WANG YUN:

Bows with clasped hands.

Greetings!

LU PU:

Greetings!

They both gesture to cross the threshold to enter the house.

WANG:

Please sit down.

They both sit. Wang Yün *on the left and* Lü Pu *behind the table, facing the audience.*

LU PU:

I've come here purposely to thank you for the beautiful golden headdress, which adds grandeur and pomp to my appearance.

WANG:

The recent defeat of Ts'ao Ts'ao and Liu Pei[2] was certainly due to your efforts and wonderful fighting tactics.

LU PU:

Thank you for the compliment.

WANG:

I have prepared a feast to welcome you and celebrate your victory.

LU PU:

My lord, you are the Minister of Education, while I am only an aide to the Prime Minister. I don't deserve such courtesy!

WANG:

You are the greatest hero in the empire, and I respect you not for your position as a general but for your valor and ability.

LU PU:

It is very kind of you to say so.

From the left, enter slave girls in beautiful attire to pour wine.

WANG:

To the slave girls:

Serve wine.

To Lü Pu.

It is said that Ts'ao Ts'ao and Liu Pei were running away as fast as their horses could carry them when they heard of your coming to the Tiger Pen Pass. I wish I had been there to see the excitement with my own eyes. Will you tell me how it happened?

---

2. These two famous men later became kings of two of The Three Kingdoms. Ts'ao Ts'ao, the character on the Capital Opera stage who always wears the white-painted face, became king of the state of Wei, while Liu Pei ruled the state of Shu.

LU PU:

It was a smashing victory. Ts'ao Ts'ao and Liu Pei gathered their troops and disappeared like smoke, clouds. You can see now what heroes they are! It was a simple–an easy–victory! You should have seen them run like rabbits for their lives! What a joke!

The Servant *enters from the right.*

SERVANT:

My lord, a messenger from the Western Palace is here to call you to a conference.

WANG:

All right.

Exit the Servant *to right.*

How do you like the golden headdress I sent you?

LU PU:

It is exactly like the one I lost on the battlefield. Who made it?

WANG:

Why, my daughter made it with her own hands.

LU PU:

Surprised.

Your daughter? What a smart girl! Why don't you let me have the pleasure of meeting her?

WANG:

All right, let me ask her to come out.

Calling to the right–

Tiao Ch'an, where are you?

TIAO CH'AN:

Off stage.

Coming.

Tiao Ch'an *enters from the left. She is now in a gorgeous dress of yellow satin.*

The white cloud is heartless fog
That is led out by the spring breeze.
Approaches Wang Yün.
Father, I am here.

WANG:
This is General Lü Pu, the great hero.

TIAO CH'AN:
Goes to Lü Pu *and bows.*

LU PU:
Stands up and bows with clasped hands.
My greetings, Miss.

WANG:
My child, go and thank the General for his constant kind help at court.

TIAO CH'AN:
Oh yes, General, you have always helped and done favors for my father at court. I am very grateful to you.
Kowtows.

LU PU:
Please don't mention it.

WANG:
Now, my child, pour a cup of wine to show your respects.

LU PU:
Oh no, allow me to help myself.

WANG:
Let her do it for you . . .

LU PU:
Why don't you sit down and join us?

TIAO CH'AN:

Blushes and lowers her head.

WANG:

My child, the General is one of my closest friends, so it is perfectly proper for you to sit down.

LU PU:

Oh yes, please sit down. The Minister and I are great friends. There is no harm. It is proper, indeed. Please do sit down.

Tiao Ch'an *seats herself on* Lü Pu's *right, while* Lü Pu *stares, dazzled by her beauty.*

WANG:

To your health.

Reenter the Servant *from the right.*

SERVANT:

The messenger is here again to ask you to go to the Western Palace.

WANG:

How dare you come in while the young lady is here?

SERVANT:

Because the messenger has come several times and said it is very urgent.

WANG:

Go out at once.

Exit the Servant;

LU PU:

What's the matter? Who wants to see you?

WANG:

Ah, It's your father who wants to confer with me. The servant should not have disturbed me while I am entertaining such a distinguished guest.

LU PU:

Since you are not free, I'd better be going.

WANG:

How can you talk about going when we haven't yet finished a pot of wine! I'm sure it won't take me long to confer with the Prime Minister. My dear child, while I'm away, do entertain the General and make him feel at home and drink more.

LU PU:

Oh, it isn't right!

WANG:

I just told you–we're great friends. What's wrong with that? Let me present a toast before I go. Ai-ya, the wine is cold!

A slave girl comes to bring a pot of hot wine and then exits.

Pardon me, and goodbye for the moment.

They all rise.

LU PU:

Goodbye–see you in a moment.

Exit Wang Yün *to the left.*

Please do sit down.

They both sit.

TIAO CH'AN:

Let me pour you another cup of hot wine.

LU PU:

Miss, may I ask what your name is?

TIAO CH'AN:

Tiao Ch'an is my name.

LU PU:

Do you read?

TIAO CH'AN:

Yes, a little.

LU PU:

For a girl, the more ignorant the better. How old are you?

TIAO CH'AN:

Two times nine.

LU PU:

Are you engaged to anyone?

TIAO CH'AN:

Blushing.

Not yet.

LU PU:

You are young–just the age to get married!

TIAO CH'AN:

In *The Book of Changes*[3] *it* says: "Happier is the person who marries late."

LU PU:

Miss, since you know what *The Book of Changes* says, do you know the line in *The Book of Poetry*[4] that reads: "A gentleman likes to woo a beautiful and virtuous girl?"

TIAO CH'AN:

There is truth in what you say, but I have not met a great hero as yet.

LU PU:

Well spoken. But think a little about me! I–Lü Pu–have fought many battles and never lost *one!* No one has been my equal on the battlefield. From the recent victory before the Tiger Pen Pass, everybody knows my valor and skill–three attacks at T'ao Yüan and the army of the eighteen great nobles flew apart like scattering chickens in face of an attack from an eagle. They

---

3. *The Book of Changes* and *The Book of Poetry* are among the earliest books of China. It is said to have been Confucius (551-479 B.C.) who reduced the number of poems in *The Book of Poetry* from three thousand to three hundred fifty, and completed the editing of these two famous books in the form in which they have come down to us.
4. A famous beauty of the 5th Century B.C. From a humble family, *Hsi Shih* (西施) was taken and trained by the king of Yueh and afterward used to seduce the king of Wu and cause his defeat.

cringed with fear at the sound of my name! Now, do you consider me a hero?

Wang Yün *peeps from upstage left.*

TIAO CH'AN:

At the sound of your name?

LU PU:

Yes, at the sound of my name! Am I not a hero?

TIAO CH'AN:

Of course, you are. You are the greatest of heroes. You have no equal!

LU PU:

Since I am a hero, you ought to accept.

TIAO CH'AN:

Accept what?

LU PU:

Accept my proposal of marriage.

Wang Yün *coughs and reenters.*

WANG:

Oh, pardon me, pardon me, General. Pardon me for leaving you like this.

Tiao Ch'an *looks coyly at* Lü Pu.

To Tiao Ch'an:

Why are you still here? Ah, General, this is going too far! Are you *drunk?*

Exit Tiao Ch'an *to the left.*

LU PU:

Pretends to be drunk.

Yes, I am drunk . . . very drunk.

WANG:

I'm sorry I had to leave you alone with my daughter.

LU PU:

There's nothing to be sorry about. It's been a pleasure–a pleasure! I enjoyed your daughter's company immensely. She is like a lovely peach–so intelligent, so beautiful, so . . .

WANG:

Thank you for the complimen

LU PU:

Is she engaged to anyone?

WANG:

No, she isn't. Since she's our only child, she's a little spoiled. She doesn't want to marry anyone but a hero!

Pauses.

My dear General, if you care to take her for a wife, I would be glad to present her to you.

LU PU:

Now, Your Excellency, please don't tease me!

WANG:

You have been doing favors for me at court for a long time and I have never had a chance to reciprocate your kindness. This is my opportunity. Why would I tease you?

LU PU:

I am very grateful to you.

WANG:

Let's announce the engagement today, and tomorrow we'll set a date for the wedding. In the meantime, I shall prepare my daughter's dowry to be sent to your house.

LU PU:

When is the wedding day?

WANG:

Today is the 13th–it's a lucky day!

LU PU:

Good, let's make it today.

WANG:

Not enough time to prepare. Tomorrow is the 14th.

LU PU:

All right, tomorrow then.

WANG:

The 14th is the anniversary of the death of my father.

LU PU:

That doesn't matter.

WANG:

But I also am inviting the Prime Minister to dinner tomorrow. However, the 15th can be the happy day–a day of family reunion–so I will personally send her to your palace on that day.

LU PU:

Oh, how wonderful to get married! I will henceforth try my utmost to fight with even greater valor. Father-in-law, accept my salutations!

Bows with clasped hands.

WANG:

My salutations to the lucky day before us!

Bows before the audience.

LU PU:

I am like a dragon, to take a bride on the Midautumn Festival.

WANG:

Fate brings together the two who are destined to marry even though they are thousands of miles apart!

LU PU:

It's fate again that prevents two people from getting married even though they often see each other. For the time being, father-in-law, farewell!

To the attendants off stage:

Lead the horse in.

Exit Lü Pu *to the right.*

Wang's Servant *quietly enters from the left.*

WANG:

Laughing–

What a joke! Lao Chang! Go and invite the Prime Minister to dinner tomorrow.

SERVANT:

Yes, my lord.

Exit the Servant *to the right.*

WANG:

The marvelous design of the tender snare is to lure the traitor with the feminine air! Ha-ha! Ha-ha!

Exit to upstage left.

SCENE FOUR

The same scene.

Tung Cho enters with attendants from upstage right, while Wang Yün enters from upstage left. They meet downstage center and gesture to enter the house. The attendants exit to right.

Tung Cho *sits in the center facing the audience,*

feasting, while Wang Yün *sit on the left.*

TUNG CHO:

All the other high officials are against me, except you. So when I am emperor, you shall be my Prime Minister.

WANG YUN:

Thank you, Your Excellency.

TUNG:

Since we have eaten, what do you say to some . . . entertainment . er . . . some dancing . . .

WANG:

To Servant:

Ask Tiao Ch'an to come here at once.

Enter Tiao Ch'an *from the left. She is now in a light-pink dress and is more beautiful than before.*

TIAO CH'AN:

Comes to downstage left.

My father asks me to dance and sing before the Prime Minister.

Goes to Wang and bows.

WANG:

Greet His Excellency, my child.

TIAO CH'AN:

I kowtow to Your Excellency.

Kowtows.

TUNG:

Arise, oh . . . oh . . .

Looks hungrily at Tiao Ch'an *as* Tiao Ch'an *rises.*

WANG:

Dance, sing, and pour wine for His Excellency.

TIAO CH'AN:

Yes, master.

Sings and dances.

A silver wine jar in my hand
To pour wine into a cup of jade.
Please, Your Excellency, drink your fill.
Then listen to my song of love.
And feast your eyes on my dance of the fairies,

And I'll come back again to present
To you this wine of fragrance.

TUNG:

Beautiful, beautiful!

Stroking his beard.

TIAO CH'AN:

Smiles sweetly and continues to sing.

Just a smile, a flirtatious smile,
Will take him away
From the affairs of the state.
Just a glance–a sweet glance–
Will keep his heart
Beating, beating away
To the land of love and dreams!

TUNG:

Oh . . beautiful!

TIAO CH'AN:

Continues.

Shall I make him
Lose his wits, or overwhelm
Him with beauty and love?

Gracefully dances up to Tung Cho. *Pours wine.*

Your Excellency, have another cup of wine.

TUNG:

All right, I'll have another.

drinks.

TIAO CH'AN:

Oh, Your Excellency, have another one.

TUNG:

Ah, I really can't take another one, but since you insist , . . all right . . . I'll have another.

Drinks.

Ah, my dear Minister, what is her name?

WANG:

Tiao Ch'an.

TUNG:

Good, good, good. Tiao Ch'an is a beautiful name, as beautiful as the person. She is as alluring as Hsi Shih.[5]

Aside.

If I ever have the fortune to possess such a beautiful girl, I shall not live in vain. Let me tempt her.

Aloud to Wang Yün–

My dear Minister, do you know my biggest problem?

WANG:

No, I'm sorry I don't.

TUNG:

I want to choose a beautiful girl who can dance and sing.

WANG:

What for?

TUNG:

Since I have gold and silver piled up as high as the mountains, I want a living, breathing picture to entertain and serve me . . .

WANG:

So that's your problem.

Pause.

Er . . . if Your Excellency does not mind the homeliness of my slave girl, may I present her to you? At least she can sing and dance.

---

5. A famous beauty of the 5th Century B.C. From a humble family, *Hsi Shih* (西施) was taken and trained by the king of Yueh and afterward used to seduce the king of Wu and cause his defeat.

TUNG:

Pleased.

I hope you are not making fun of me.

WANG:

Ah, Your Excellency, how dare I? I'm greatly indebted to you for all the favors you have bestowed upon me. A girl means nothing, compared to your favors!

TUNG:

Please accept my thanks, my good Minister.

WANG:

Don't mention it, Your Excellency. Although Tiao Ch'an is a slave girl, we have been treating her like our own daughter ever since she came to our house. So I hope you will not treat her ill and pardon her if she does any wrong.

TUNG:

How could I ever mistreat her! When I am emperor, you shall be the emperor's father-in-law!

WANG:

All I pray is that my girl shall have a good home.

TUNG:

What about asking your girl to come back with me right now?

WANG:

Let me ask for her opinion first.

To Tiao Ch'an:

Would you be willing to go with the Prime Minister?

TIAO CH'AN:

If this is your order, how dare I disobey? Besides, it's an honor to be the wife of the Prime Minister. All I want to do is to serve him well.

TUNG:

Well said, my girl.

WANG:

Since that's the case, change and make yourself beautiful so that you can follow His Excellency to his palace.

TIAO CH'AN:

Yes, my lord.

Exit Tiao Ch'an *to the left.*

TUNG:

Wonderful! Bravo!

WANG:

To the attendants off stage:

Get the carriages ready.

Reenter Tiao Ch'an *in a beautiful bright-red gown and a long red cape.*

To Tiao Ch'an:

Now you are leaving me for the Prime Minister's Palace. Remember to serve him well, my child.

TIAO CH'AN:

Yes, I will, my lord.

TUNG:

Rushing eagerly toward Tiao Ch'an–

Allow me to help you into the carriage. Be careful, my dear.

Tung Cho *and* Tiao Ch'an *walk between two flags painted with wheels and held by an attendant at the back.*

They exit to upstage right.

TUNG:

Off stage.

To the palace!

WANG:

Farewell! Farewell!

He laughs heartily.
Exit to left.

SCENE FIVE

SCENE FIVE

Same scene, the next morning.
Wang Yün *is sitting in front of a table on stage center, alone reading when* Lü Pu *rushes in angrily from the right.*

LU PU:

You old swindler, you! Why did you double-cross me? You promised me your daughter yesterday, and now you have married her off to the Prime Minister as a concubine. Ah-pei!

Spits at Wang Yün.

WANG YUN:

Rising–

General, calm yourself and listen to me. The Prime Minister came here yesterday and asked me about your engagement to my daughter. I had to order her to come out and meet him. Then he said it was the proper time to take the bride home for you, my General. As His Excellency came personally to fetch your bride, how could I refuse? How could I prevent it? Could I deny that Tiao Ch'an wasn't engaged to you? Could I?

LU PU:

Alas, Your Excellency, he himself has taken her as his concubine.

WANG:

Ai-ya, what a disgrace! How could he ever do such an outrageous thing? How beastly of him! Come over here.

Spits at Lü Pu.

Pei! My poor daughter, I have promised to marry you to a man of your dreams–a hero. Who would have thought he was also a coward and a good-for-nothing?

LU PU:

I swear I will be no man if I do not marry this girl. Your Excellency, I apologize for having misjudged you. I deserve my punishment whenever you want it. In the meantime, farewell!

To the attendants off stage, left:

My horse, bring my horse!

Lü Pu *exits in a hurry to the right.*

WANG:

Ha, now this will be a tender snare for both father and son!

Exit to left.

SCENE SIX

The back garden in Tung Cho's *Palace*

Late afternoon.

In the center, a beautiful pavilion, with a tablet over it on which is written "Phoenix Pavilion." A lotus pond is nearby, spanned by a curved red wooden bridge. On the left, a path leads to the other part of the garden. We can also see many trees and flowers in our imagination. A willow tree upstage shades the pavilion. On the left is a covered corridor that leads to the house. But what we actually see is almost a bare stage with a table and a chair in front of it.

Enter Lü Pu *from the right. He is waiting impatiently in the pavilion for* Tiao Ch'an, *who runs gracefully in from upstage left through the corridor.*

LU PU:

Ah, at last you are here! Tiao Ch'an!

TIAO CH'AN:

I had to ask you to come to this pavilion. This is the only place that is private enough. Why hadn't you come to see me? You know how much I love you and how much I have been suffering with that old beast.

LU PU:

He doesn't allow me to come to the inner rooms any more since you came.

He's jealous of me. Today he went into court for the first time in weeks to see the Emperor. So I seized the chance, slipped out and galloped back here as fast as I could to see you, my dear.

Pause.

Oh, my wife! How I long for you!

Comes near her.

TIAO CH'AN:

Ugh! Your wife! You call yourself a hero! And yet such a coward! Are you willing to wear horns without a struggle? Since you are so frightened of that old bandit, I can never hope to see the day of freedom.

Weeps.

LU PU:

Don't cry, my dear; let me think of a way to save you.

TIAO CH'AN:

Your name was known to be as terrific as thunder and lightning when I was at home. Everyone knew you were the greatest hero. Who would ever imagine that you are now a good-for-nothing weakling?

LU PU:

Ai-ya! I swear I am no man if I cannot take you for my wife!

Enter Tung Cho *from the left. Seeing him,* Tiao Ch'an *pretends to jump into the pond, but* Lü Pu *rushes to her and holds her back.*

TUNG CHO:

You bastard, you! How dare you seduce my beloved concubine! I knew your trick, so I rushed back from the court.

Lü Pu *starts to run to the right and crosses the bridge, while* Tung Cho *pulls out his sword and follows.*

Stop, you rascal! You can't escape!

Exit Lü Pu *to upstage right, with* Tung Cho *running after him.*

TIAO CH'AN:

Oh, I don't know what to think. For loyalty's sake, I should wish Tung

Tiao Ch'an pretends to struggle with Lu Pu to throw herself into the pond as Tung Cho, in great fury and jealousy, attempts to kill Lu Pu.

Cho would kill Lü Pu. But somehow I feel sad—sad deep in my heart. What can it be? Can it be love?

Steps are heard.

Here the Prime Minister is back, Has he killed Lü Pu, I wonder?

Reenter Tung Cho, *furious and out of breath.*

TUNG:

Bah! Let him go. He'll answer for it someday.

Turning to Tiao Ch'an—

Ha! You shameless woman! Why did you arrange a rendezvous with your lover, Lü Pu, while I was away to see the Emperor?

TIAO CH'AN:

Oh, my lord, how can you say such a thing! I was all alone in the garden looking at the flowers, when all of a sudden Lü Pu jumped right before me! I tried to run away, but he laughed and said since he was your son, why should I be afraid of him! And then he dragged me to the Phoenix Pavilion. I was afraid he had bad intentions, so I tried to drown myself by jumping into the lotus pond. I never thought that hateful general would ever hold me in his arms! Just as I was fighting for my life, Your Excellency came to my rescue. If you had come just a tiny bit later, I would have drowned myself!

TUNG CHO:

I intend to send you to Lü Pu today. How do you like that, young lady?

TIAO CH'AN:

Ai-ya! My lord, I am already married to you. How can you give me to another? I'd rather die than leave you. Let me kill myself before your eyes.

Bangs her head against one of the imaginary pillars of the pavilion.

TUNG CHO:

Rushing to stop her—

No, no, my dear, I was only joking.

Tiao Ch'an *weeps.*

Tung Cho *sits down and pulls her onto his lap, where she leans on his shoulder, weeping.*

TIAO CH'AN:

Sweetly.

I don't want to leave you for a minute. I know who's behind all this. It's that scheming Li Su again. He planned this to help Lü Pu, his bosom friend, at the expense of your reputation and my life. Only eating him alive can satisfy my hatred for him!

TUNG CHO:

Never again will I listen to that sly ditchdigger. How can I ever part with my sweet little darling, eh?

Tries to kiss her, but she evades him and runs away. He gets up.

We'll leave here tomorrow for my home in Mei Wu County and nobody can disturb us there, not even Lü Pu, who wants to seduce you, nor Li Su, who tries to convince me that you–my lady love–will ruin my future and my "kingdom!" No one will disturb us any more. We shall be alone all day and do nothing but watch the flowers and listen to the lovebirds sing.

They both go out to upstage left.

SCENE SEVEN

The next day.
Before the imaginary gate of Tung Cho's *mansion in Mei Wu County.*
There are also imaginary trees and rocks on both sides of the gate.
Enter Lü Pu *and* Wang Yün *from the right.*

LU PU:

Dear father-in-law, at last we are now here in Mei Wu County before the gate of Tung Cho's mansion. I have set the plot. Our friend, Li Su, is tempting Tung Cho to go to court, making him believe that the Emperor is seriously ill and wants him to succeed to the throne. Now I am prepared to kill!

Pause.

Yet somehow I still feel uneasy about killing my father.

WANG YUN:

Your father? Let me remind you that your surname is Lü and his is Tung.

He's no more father to you than I am. Why, he was no father when he tried to kill you before Tiao Ch'an in the Phoenix Pavilion. Lü Pu, think of the sacred cause of saving and strengthening the empire of Han! What a greater hero you'll be after you have killed the usurper–the traitor–of Han! Your name will live for generations to come. And what's more–think of poor Tiao Ch'an–suffering from that old monster's pestering while her heart is with you all the time. You will be doubly rewarded by the gratitude of Tiao Ch'an and the people of the empire.

LU PU:

You are right, my lord. I am determined! My heart is set. He thinks he'll be emperor, eh! When our friend, Li Su, leads him out, I will approach him and tear out his beastly heart!

Voices are heard off stage.

Come, let us hide behind this rock.

They hide behind an imaginary big rock on the right. Voices are heard. Cymbals and drums are sounded. From upstage right enter Li Su, *a man about twenty-six, dressed in armor, leads in a group of soldiers beating the drums and cymbals to herald the arrival of the emperor. They walk across the stage and exit to the left.*

Enter from the right, Tung Cho, *followed by* Tiao Ch'an *and attendants.*

TUNG:

I dreamed there was a dragon[6] over my body last night, and the dream has come true. Now I am really emperor. After my coronation, I'll come back for you. Ah, my dear, I have had the best time of my life with you for the last few days. Farewell–farewell for a day–my dear queen.

Reenter Li Su *from the left.*

To Li Su:

Is the carriage ready?

LI SU:

Yes, Your Majesty.

---

6. The dragon is the symbol of the emperor.

TUNG:

What did Wang Yün say about my being made emperor?

LI SU:

He is very happy about it and is now making preparations for the welcome.

TUNG:

Aside.

My heart is burning—burning to be emperor . . . and yet afraid of dangerous opposition. Where is Lü Pu? It doesn't seem safe to go to the capital without my strong son as bodyguard.

Cries.

Lü Pu! Lü Pu!

Takes a few steps forward.

Lü Pu!

Lü Pu *springs up from behind the rock with sword in hand and jumps at* Tung Cho.

LU PU:

Here I am, you dirty usurper, you—usurper of an empire and of my wife! Here's your reward!

Stabs Tung Cho.

TUNG CHO:

Ah, my son, my son! So it's you . . . you have stopped me from taking the throne.

Groans and falls on the ground.

Screams are heard.

LU PU:

Comrades and friends, the traitor to the House of Han is dead. Long live the Emperor! Long live our freedom!

Tiao Ch'an *rushes forward into the arms of* Lü Pu *and they embrace.*

(CURTAIN)

TWICE A BRIDE

(Hung Luan Hsi)

Twice a Bride is a typical folk story with which every Chinese is familiar. Mo Chi, a poor scholar, meets and marries the daughter of the Chief of Beggars. After he has achieved success–thanks to his wife's unselfish efforts–Mo Chi gets rid of her by tossing her into a river. He thinks that she is drowned, but she is saved by the Governor of Kiangsi, who takes her into his home and treats her as his own daughter. To teach him a lesson, the Governor arranges for Mo Chi to marry his adopted daughter. Mo Chi does not suspect she could be his first wife and is gratified to marry so well. The denouement comes after the wedding (Chinese brides in arranged marriages always wore a piece of red silk over their heads and faces until reaching the bridal chamber) when she punishes him thoroughly. Then they decide to forget the past and renew their marriage.

The reader will discover quickly that *Twice a Bride* does not have the depth or drama of the two previous plays. It is more a burlesque of life than a description of it. Perhaps it could be described best as a Chinese morality play. And the moral stands out here in broad strokes of rustic humor: ingratitude will be punished.

This is borne out by the Chinese name, *Hung Luan Hsi* (鴻 鸞 禧), which means "Vast Marital Felicity," or "May You Have Great Marital Joy." One cannot help smiling at the irony of this greeting to the grossly selfish groom, who is obviously stuck for life with a bride who has the psychological and moral whip hand over him, whereas the positions could have been reversed had he displayed even a modicum of gratitude.

This play was produced by the University of Hawaii Theatre Group and the Department of Drama and Theatre in Honolulu in April, 1963. For this production, I added four scenes to the five scenes in the version in the first edition of this book. There are altogether 28 characters of all the different role types appearing in the nine scenes.

The performances under the direction of Daniel S.P. Yang were so enchanting and fascinating that it was sent on a tour to the neighboring islands in May of the same year.

This play was also presented by the Hanover College Theatre, Indiana, in conjunction with the Institute on China, under the direction of John C. Jeorse in March, 1967. It too, enjoyed great success.

TWICE A BRIDE

Characters

* *MO CHI*................................*A Young scholar; aged 20*
(莫 稽)

* *CHIN SUNG* ....*Chief of Beggars in the city of Lin-an; aged 65*
(金 松)

* *YU NU*........................*daughter of Chin Sung; aged 16*
(玉 奴)

* *LAO ERH*..................*subordinate beggar to Chin Sung; aged 40*
(老 二)

* *LIN JUN* ....*Governor of Kiangsi Province; aged 60*
(林 潤)

* *MADAME LIN*...........................*wife of Lin Jun; aged 60*

* *THE GOD OF HAPPINESS*

* *MINOR OFFICIAL aged 30*

* *BUTLER aged 40*

* *Two MAIDS*
Two ANGELS
Two BEGGARS (played by two ANGELS)
RIVER GOD (played by one of the ANGELS)

* *MESSENGER*

* *OARSMAN (for both LIN JUN and MO CHI)*
Four LUNG T'AO (attendants; both for MO CHI and for LIN JUN)
Property Man

Altogether 28 characters appear in this play.
Could be reduced into 20 with doubling.

* *represents speaking part.*

SCENE ONE

The back of the stage represents the interior of Chin Sung's hut. A table is in the center with two chairs on either side. The space between the footlights and the back of the stage is the street.

Enter the Angel of Happiness *from the left with two angels, who hold banners decorated with clouds to show they are walking on clouds in the sky.*

Angel of Happiness:

I am the Angel of Happiness. By the order of Heaven, I am to set the scene for Yu Nu and Mo Chi to meet, for they are destined to be married.

He climbs up on the table and gestures to look afar.

I can see Mo Chi coming from a distance.

Mo Chi, *a scholarly young man in tatters, enters from the right.*

MO CHI:

Ou-o-o-o! How cold it is! I'm trembling and shivering. How can I go on with an empty stomach and no coat on my back?

To the audience

I am your humble servant, Mo Chi, a scholar, and as poor as a church mouse, for I was left an orphan when I was very young. I'm forced to beg from house to house now to keep myself alive. For the past three days I haven't tasted food and I'm on the verge of starvation. Oh, Heaven, what good is all my learning without a home, food, and clothing? When will fortune cast favor upon me, I wonder?

Snow falls and Mo Chi *faints and falls down on the doorstep of* Chin Sung's *hut.*

Angel of Happiness:

Now, Mo Chi, that's right! Lie on the doorstep and someone will come to take care of you. Angels, let's go back to heaven.

Angel of Happiness *and* the angels *go out to the left.*

The table is removed by the property man. Enter Yu Nu *from the right,*

YU NU:

I am as young as the spring,
Two times eight is my age-ring.
I was born and brought up in a poor family,
But I am living beautifully and happily.
Both sweetness and light there are in life.
Wealth and nobility,
Lowliness and poverty
Are the free choices of Fate for man.
Therefore, I, Yu Nu,
Am perfectly satisfied
To be poor and humble
Rather than rich and noble.

Speaks.

My name is Yu Nu, and my father is Chin Sung, the Chief of Beggars. He has been out helping at a friend's wedding ever since dawn. I've been left all by myself. Oh, I feel so lonesome-- so very lonesome.

Yu Nu *sings* Hsi-P'i-Yuan-Pan *and opens the door.*

Ai-ya! A young man! Hey, you, what are you doing in front of my door? Hey, wake up! Wake up!

Pushes and shakes him.

MO CHI:

Groaning

Ouch! Oooo-oo!

Yu Nu:

Oh, he's alive!

MO CHI:

(*Waking up)* It's a woman!

Yu Nu:

No, I'm not a woman--I'm only a girl. Who are you and what are you doing on my doorstep?

MO CHI:

I'm starving. I haven't tasted food for three days and I'm dying from cold. I . . . I can't take another step!

YU NU:

That's too bad. I have some soybean milk inside. Would you like to have some?

MO CHI:

Yes, I'm very much obliged, Miss.

YU NU:

It's very cold out here. Come on in and have some hot soup.

MO CHI:

Oh, my feet are so frozen and numb I cannot walk.

YU NU:

Must I carry you in?

MO CHI:

I think I can crawl in.

YU NU:

Crawl in, then!

Mo Chi *crawls up the doorstep into the house and sits on the floor, at the right of the audience.*

YU NU:

Wait here while I go in and get you some hot soybean soup.
(*Aside)* Poor man, trembling and shivering from hunger and cold.
To do a good deed may bring me good fortune.

To Mo Chi.

You just wait a minute.

Exit left through the curtained door at the back.

MO CHI:

It's really Heaven's blessing that I've met such a kind girl.
She's saving my life!

Enter Chin Sung *upstage right.*

CHIN SUNG:

I am the Chief of Beggars,
An expert in commanding my men
To beg leftovers
For me and my daughter.

Sees Mo Chi.

Hey you! The sight of another beggar sets me in a rage!

MO CHI:

Oh, so my honorable sir is back.

CHIN SUNG:

Honorable sewer? What's so honorable in a sewer?
It's as dirty as a gutter. Who are you, anyway?

MO CHI:

I'm a cold, hungry man . . . a man in despair!

CHIN SUNG:

A man in despair? A cold and hungry man is naturally a beggar.
Don't you know who I am? Begging from me is like trying to snatch food from a tiger's mouth!

MO CHI:

I didn't come in here of my own accord, sir.

CHIN SUNG:

Ah-ha! you didn't come here of your own accord, eh?
Did I send you a formal invitation to come?

MO CHI:

There's a girl here who asked me to come in.

CHIN SUNG:

A girl here asked you to come in? Oho! Don't make me laugh!
Don't you dare insult our house. We are respectable people.
I'll ask her myself. If you're lying, I'll punish you!

Yu Nu, come here!

Enter Yu Nu *with a bowl in her hand.*

Yu Nu *sings* Hsi-P'i-Yiao-Pan

YU NU:

Father, so you are back at last! Did you have a nice time at the wedding?

CHIN SUNG:

You! You've disgraced me and my family name!

YU NU:

Why are you so angry? Is anything wrong?

CHIN SUNG:

Now, let me ask you. I was out for only a short time and you have already taken a man into the house. What will people say? You have ruined completely my reputation. Damn you!

YU NU:

Oh, so that's why you are angry! Just because of that man in our house? Now don't be angry with me. Let me explain.

CHIN SUNG:

Hurry up and explain.

YU NU:

You were out helping your friend with his wedding since dawn and I was worried when you didn't come back in the late afternoon. So I went to have a look. I saw this fellow lying on the doorstep. He told me he was hungry and cold. We have a lot of soybean soup in our house and I wanted to save him from starvation. Now, Father, is helping the hungry and cold disgraceful?

CHIN SUNG:

Laughing

The older I am, the more stupid I get. I'm sorry I blamed you for doing a good deed, my dear girl. Now, where is the soup?

YU NU:

It's probably cold by now.

MO CHI:

I don't mind, honorable sir.

CHIN SUNG:

Oh, he doesn't mind, Yu Nu. Give him some soup.

Yu Nu *gives him the bowl.*

MO CHI:

Drinks and empties the bowl.

May I have some more, honorable sir?

CHIN SUNG:

We have no more.

MO CHI:

Drops the bowl on the floor. It breaks.

I feel much better after the bowl of soup. Kind people like you are rare in this world. Now let me show my gratitude to you for saving my life, honorable sir.

CHIN SUNG:

Let me give you a good hard beating!

YU NU:

Why, Father, why do you want to beat him?

CHIN SUNG:

That ungrateful rat! He not only drank our soup without a word of thanks but keeps on calling me horrible sewer.

MO CHI:

That's not true. You misunderstood my words. I address you as honorable sir. Honorable sir means a gentlemen of distinction–not horrible sewer!

CHIN SUNG:

Ah, now I understand–honorable sir, a gentleman of distinction.
Good, good. Are you still hungry and cold?

MO CHI:

No, I am neither hungry nor cold. I feel find now . . . just fine.

CHIN SUNG:

Well, what are you waiting for?

MO CHI:

All right, I'll go.

YU NU:

Oh, come back!

Mo Chi *approaches* Yu Nu.

CHIN SUNG:

Why did you call him back?

YU NU:

I want to ask him a question.

Turns to Mo Chi.

You did thank my father, but what about me?

MO CHI:

I am sorry, Miss, I forgot.

Bows.

Thank you for saving my life.

YU NU:

Father, why don't you ask him to leave his name and address so that when he makes his fortune, he'll be able to return our kindness.

CHIN SUNG:

What a smart girl you are! All right, let me ask him.

To Mo Chi:

What is your name, and where do you live?

MO CHI:

My surname is Mo, my given name is Chi, and I am a scholar in this city.

YU NU:

Pleased and excited

Father, did you hear that? He is a scholar.

CHIN SUNG:

It's a good thing he's a scholar of the lowest degree. If he were a professor he would have broken my stove instead of the soup bowl!

YU NU:

Poor man, I feel so sorry for him. We have some leftovers your beggar friends have given us; let me give him some before he leaves.

CHIN SUNG:

I wanted to eat them myself with my wine.

YU NU:

I'll save some delicious tidbits for you–don't worry.

To Mo Chi:

Please don't go!

Smiles at him and exits.

MO CHI:

His eyes follow Yü Nu *as she leaves, and he smiles to himself.*

I'm not leaving this time. I'm going to stay.

CHIN SUNG:

To audience

This time it looks as though he'll get a permanent meal ticket from me!

To Mo Chi:

Sit down, please sit down.

They both sit, Chin Sung *on the right of the table and* Mo Chi *on the left.*

We know your name, but you haven't asked for mine.

MO CHI:

That's true. May I know your name, honorable sir?

CHIN SUNG:

Surname is Chin and given name is Sung.

MO CHI:

O, sir, *chin* means the gold that fills up the house, and *sung* is the evergreen pine. That is wealth and prosperity forever. What a refined name! Sir Chin, who is the young lady living here with you?

CHIN SUNG:

She's my daughter.

MO CHI:

Oh, the honorable lady of the house! What's her name?

CHIN SUNG:

Yü Nu.

MO CHI:

Writes the name on his palm.

Yü is jade, a lovely precious stone, and *nu* is a young girl. So it means jade girl, the lovely girl. Oh, what an exquisite and elegant name!

Licks his palm and swallows.

CHIN SUNG:

What are you doing that for? Would you like to devour her?

MO CHI:

So that I can remember the name forever and ever.

CHIN SUNG:

May I be excused for a minute?

Walks downstage right. Aside.

This young man, Mo Chi, seems to be very learned. I'd better take him for my son-in-law so that I may live with him when I get old and my dear daughter will be taken care of.

Goes back to his seat and to Mo Chi.

I want to ask you something.

MO CHI:

Honorable sir, if you have any advice for me, please do not hesitate to say so.

CHIN SUNG:

I have a daughter and I've planned to . . to . . .

MO CHI:

Planned to do what, sir?

Moves his chair closer to Chin Sung.

CHIN SUNG:

To . . . to . . . er . . .

Moves away from Mo Chi *to the right.*

MO CHI:

Honorable sir, what are you planning to do?

Moves closer to Chin Sung.

CHIN SUNG:

Rises in disgust.

I am planning to beat you up!

They move their chairs back to the center.

It's so hard to say. What I really want to tell you is this. I plan to make you my son-in-law. How do you like that?

MO CHI:

May I be excused?

Goes downstage left and says to himself.

Ai-ya! That Yü Nu–she is the daughter of the Chief of Beggars! How can I take her for a wife! Oh, well, since now I haven't got a home or money, I have to consent for the time being. Someday when I find my fortune, I'll try to get rid of her.

Returns to his seat.

Oh, Sir Chin, I'd be greatly honored to be your son-in-law, but I'm too poor for your daughter.

CHIN SUNG:

When you are married to my daughter, you belong to the family. You say you are poor? We don't have any money either, so let's bluff our way along. Can you do that?

MO CHI:

I'm an expert at that!

They both bring their chairs downstage center and sit down.

CHIN SUNG:

In that case, you begin bluffing right now.

MO CHI:

Ah, honorable father-in-law, I have prepared everything for the wedding.

CHIN SUNG:

Ah, my son-in-law, your honor, what have you prepared?

MO CHI:

Here are a thousand taels of gold, a hundred rolls of colored silk, a bridal crown, a ceremonial robe and cape. I wish you would accept my humble gifts, honorable father-in-law.

CHIN SUNG:

The bride will need the bridal crown, the ceremonial robe and cape, but we must return to you the thousand taels of gold and the hundred rolls of colored silk.

MO CHI:

Oh, no, no!

Looks at his ragged gown.

Ai-ya! I've torn another piece of my tatters!

CHIN SUNG:

I've also prepared something for the wedding.

MO CHI:

What have you prepared, honorable father-in-law?

CHIN SUNG:

Here are an ivory bed, a golden chamber pot, a silver night stool, and a hundred sets of silk bedding for Yü Nu's dowry.

MO CHI:

Why do you give us so many sets of bedding, may I ask, honorable father-in-law?

CHIN SUNG:

My son, someday in case you have no other business to do, you will be able to establish a little hotel.

MO CHI:

I accept the ivory bed with heartfelt gratitude, but I must return half of the sets of bedding.

CHIN SUNG:

Oh, no, you must keep them all.

MO CHI:

In the course of make-believe, he tears another piece of his tattered gown.

Oh, heavens! There goes another piece of my precious rags!

Lao Erh, *a subordinate beggar, with two beggars, enter upstage right. He knocks at the imaginary door of* Chin Sung's *hut.*

LAO ERH:

Big brother Chin Sung, are you home?

CHIN SUNG:

Comes to the doorstep and gestures to open the door.

Oh, what a coincidence! I am about to marry my daughter to a scholar.

To Mo Chi:

Now, pay your respects to this honorable gentleman, Uncle Lao Erh.

MO CHI:

Bows

My salutations to you, my honorable Uncle Lao Erh.

LAO ERH:

Congratulations! When is the lucky day?

CHIN SUNG:

Today is the lucky day. Do you have anything to dress up the bridegroom?

LAO ERH:

Searches his capacious pockets and takes out a pair of red trousers.

Yes, here's a pair of trousers.

CHIN SUNG:

That's fine, Put them on.

Lao Erh *helps* Mo Chi *put them over his shoulders, with the legs in front.*

How about a piece of red cloth for the bridal veil?

LAO ERH:

Produces a piece of tattered red cloth.

Will this do?

CHIN SUNG:

Admirably!

Takes the cloth.

I'll go in and bring the bride out while you attend to the bridegroom.

Chin Sung *exits right and then reenters, supporting* Yü Nu, *whose head is now covered with the red cloth and who walks with her head lowered like all Chinese brides. They place the bride and groom side by side, facing the audience.*

LAO ERH:

In a ceremonial tone

One bow, another bow, and then another bow.

The bride and groom bow accordingly.

A piece of fragrant wood,
Carved, fit to be a saddle.
Climb up, my newlyweds,
And tread the steps
Onward to the Road of Peace,
Prosperity, and Happiness!

Ceremonial music, flourish.

Bride and groom, salute each other.

They bow.

Now to the bridal chamber.

Chin Sung, *supporting* Yü Nu, *exits upstage right, followed by* Mo Chi, *A minute later,* Chin Sung *reenters.*

LAO ERH:

Congratulations, my Chief! The ceremony is now over, so we'd better be going.

CHIN SUNG:

Don't go—the feast has not yet begun. There are still some leftovers which we can enjoy together.

LAO ERH:

In that case, we'll stay.

All exit upstage left.

SCENE TWO

A month later. Morning. The set is the same as in Scene One. Enter Mo Chi *and* Yü Nu *from the right curtained door.*

MO CHI:

Cheerfully

Sings Hsi-P'i-Yuan-Pan

YU NU:

Gaily

Sings Hsi-P'i-Yuan-Pan

MO CHI:

Laughing heartily

Ha, ha, ha!

They sit, Mo Chi *on the left of the table and* Yü Nu *on the right.*

Ah, my wife, I am now warmly clothed and well-fed. Besides, I have a beautiful wife to keep me company. What more do I want of life? No more . . no more!

YU NU:

Oh, my dear husband, what are you talking about? You are still young. You ought to go to the capital to take the government examination. If you succeed again this time, you will be a high-ranking official. Why–we shall live in a grand style and will no more be beggars.

MO CHI:

Why should you speak of examinations? Am I happy enough with my sweet, sweet home?

YU NU:

If you don't want to take the examination, what are your plans, then?

MO CHI:

Of course, I have my plans. Now, my dear, when your father dies, I shall succeed him as the Chief of Beggars.

NU YU:

Oh, I see. So your great-ambition is to be the Chief of Beggars.

MO CHI:

Exactly.

YU NU:

Excellent idea!

MO CHI:

Of course, it's an idea *magnifique.*

YU NU:

I should say it's very ambitious of you.

MO CHI:

Of course, I am ambitious.

YU NU:

In a melancholy tone.

Oh, my God! Poor me, I thought I had married a great genius, a scholar, but who could have expected that my husband's dream is on the Chief of Beggar's Sceptre.

Cries

Ooooo . . . . My only wish is that he would find his fortune in the capital. Who would have expected he was but a low-down creature, too?

MO CHI:

Oh, my dear wife, don t cry any more. It's only because I love you so much that I don't want to part from you.

YU NU:

So you don't want to leave me. Now I have got it. Let's go together to the capital.

MO CHI:

All right, let's go.

He stands up and gestures to go.

YU NU:

Now, not so fast, not so fast. I have to tell my Father first.

She goes to the right and turns toward the right entrance.

Father, please come out.

Enter Chin Sung *from the right.*

CHIN SUNG:

Why did you get up so early?

MO CHI:

Good morning, my honorable Father-in-law.

He bows

CHIN SUNG:

Good morning, my honorable son-in-law.

YU NU:

Good morning, Father.

She bows

CHIN SUNG:

Oh, cut that out! Don't fuss about that damn ceremony! Sit down, my children.

They all sit in front of the table. Chin Sung *in the middle, with* Mo Chi *on his left and* Yü Nu *on his right.*

Now, tell me, what for are you up so early and why do you want to see me?

YU NU:

Father dear, hum . mm . . your son-in-law wants to tell you that . . . .

CHIN SUNG:

Come on, what does he want to tell me about?

YU NU:

He said it's about time that he should go to the capital to take the government advanced examination.

CHIN SUNG:

Very delighted

That's a grand idea! My daughter, don't you be so foolish as to hold him up! Let him go!

YU NU:

He also said . . .

CHIN SUNG:

What did he also say?

YU NU:

Hm . . mm . . he said . . hm . . said . . . .

CHIN SUNG:

God damn it! What did he say anyway?

YU NU:

Slyly and coyly

He said he didn't want to leave me.

CHIN SUNG:

Oh, so he said he didn't want to leave you. And how about you?

YU NU:

Oh . . I . . .

She covers her face with her left sleeve to indicate her shyness.

CHIN SUNG:

How do you feel about it?

YU NU:

I . . erh . . I . . will surely miss him very, very much, too.

CHIN SUNG:

He said he didn't want to leave you and you said you didn't want to let him go. Then what are you planning to do if you want him to take the examination in the capital?

NU YU:

I am . . . mm . . .

CHIN SUNG:

You are . . .

YU NU:

I am planning to go with him.

CHIN SUNG:

Ai ya ya . . who has ever heard of a dignified scholar taking his wife along to the capital for the examination?

He shakes his head in a clownish way.

YU NU:

But, Father, we are different. We are newly married and we love each other so much that we ne'er will part.

MO CHI:

That's right, Father-in-law, we are a pair of love doves that nothing can separate us.

CHIN SUNG:

So–oh, so. You are a pair of love doves that nothing can separate you. What about me? Since my old woman died, I have been taking good care of my darling daugher, Yü Nu. From a tiny peck of a thing, little by little, month in, month out, year in year out, I watched her grow. Now she has grown to a full woman. How could I expect that this dear daughter of mine came in through this door and went out through that door. Just like this.

He snaps his fingers.

She is going off with another man. And, and . . .

He cries.

I am left all alone in this world . . . all alone . . . cold and desolate . . . My old wife, oh, my old pal, where are you? Why did you have to leave me all alone, sad and lonely in this world?

He cries bitterly yet in a funny way for his whiskers and beard are moving up and down.

YU NU:

My dear Father, why are you laughing?

CHIN SUNG:

I'm *not* laughing; I'm crying.

YU NU:

There's nothing to cry about. When your son-in-law passes the government examination, he will be a high-ranking official and you will be honored and glorified with him as his father-in-law.

MO CHI:

My honorable Father-in-law, when I become a grand and mighty official, you shall have all the glory and splendor that can be found in the world. So don't you worry.

CHIN SUNG:

Enough, enough of all that bally-hoo or I'll tumble off from the balloon. Let's get down to business. Since there is no one to take care of both of you on the way, why not let me go with you.

MO CHI and YU NU:

Together

All right, let's go together.

CHIN SUNG:

But first I have to attend to some business. You two go in and pack. As soon as I am through, we'll start.

MO CHI *and* YU NU exit *to the left.*

CHIN SUNG

Goes to the right and calls.

Where are you, Lao Erh?

Enter Lao Erh, *attended by two* Beggars.

LAO ERH:

Brother Chief, what can I do for you?

CHIN SUNG:

I'll have to take my son-in-law to the capital for his examination. Now take this scepter and be my successor as the Chief of Beggars.

LAO ERH:

How can I take up this important position?
Oh, I am not smart enough–I cannot run up to it.

CHIN SUNG:

You are the one. Don't be modest.
Now salute the Royal Scepter!

Flourish as Lao Erh *bows three times to the Royal Sceptre to take over the office of the* Chief of Beggars.

Enter Mo Chi *and* Yu Nu *with bundles.*

CHIN SUNG:

Good-bye and good-bye. Peace and prosperity be with you all.

LAO ERH and BEGGARS:

Together

May nothing but good fortune be with you on the way!

Exit Chin Sung, Yu Nu *and* Mo Chi *to the right.*

LAO ERH:

Now, my fellow-men. The former Chief has bestowed this sceptre to me. From now on, I am your Chief. Do not steal chickens nor pick people's wallets. If I hear of any misbehavior from any of you, you shall be severely punished. Court is dismissed.

Exit all to the right.

SCENE THREE

The Scene is Lin Jun's *sitting room.*
Enter Lin Jun, *from the right door.*

LIN JUN:

Walks downstage and chants.

One must be loyal to the Emperor
And must be pious to one's parents.

Speaks

I am Lin Jun. By the Imperial Orders,
I was appointed Governor of Kiangsi.
I am going to start on my journey to my new post this very day.

Bulter slips in quietly from the left door and stands on Lin Jun's *left.*

LIN JUN:

Butler.

Butler *answers "aye"*

LIN JUN:

Ask Madam to come out.

BUILER:

Walks downstage, faces the right door and calls.

Please come out, Madam. The master wants to see you.

Madam Lin *enters from the right door and Bulter returns to his place.*

MADAM LIN:

Walks downstage and chants.

When the husband is a high official in the government.

The wife may enjoy all the benefits and happiness.

My lord.

LIN JUN:

Ah, Madam. I am going to start on the journey to my new post today and I want you to go with me. Order the servants to pack and to prepare the boat for sailing.

They all go out by the left door.

SCENE FOUR

A few months later. The stage represents an old temple at the outskirts of the Capital. Enter Yü Nu *from left singing* Hsi-P'i-Yiao-Pan. *Moves to Center and sits down on a chair in front of the table. A minute later,* Mo Chi *enters from upstage right, sings* Hsi-P'i-Yiao-Pan.

YU NU:

Gets up to welcome Mo Chi.

Oh, at last you're back How was the high examination.

MO CHI:

I did very well in the examination, but my stomach is now empty, Don't you have anything for me to eat?

YU NU:

My father has been out begging for food. He ought to be back by now.

Mo Chi *sits. Enter* Chin Sung *with a clapper in one hand and a bowl in the other from downstage right.*

CHIN SUNG:

Ah, I have begged half a bowl of cold boiled rice and some leftovers. It took me a whole day to get it.

YU NU:

Your son-in-law is very hungry.

CHIN SUNG:

Go ahead and eat this, my son-in-law.

MO CHI:

How about you, my father-in-law?

CHIN SUNG:

I'm not a bit hungry.

MO CHI:

How about you, Yü Nu?

YU NU:

I'm not hungry, either.

Mo Chi *eats greedily. Enter a* messenger *from the right.*

MESSENGER:

News! Good news! Who knows of a scholar Mo Chi? He has passed the examination for Chin-shih. I've looked for him all day. Who knows the whereabouts of that gentleman?

CHIN SUNG:

Comes out of the temple.

What? Mo Chi?

MESSENGER:

Yes, Lord Mo Chi. Where is he?

CHIN SUNG:

Goes back to Mo Chi, *very excited.*

You have passed–you've passed the examination!

MO CHI:

Jumps up.

What? I've passed?

Throws away the rice bowl and Chin Sung *catches it.*

Ask him to come into the temple.

Chin Sung *motions the* Messenger *to come in.*

MESSENGER:

Presenting a piece of red scroll.

Here's the announcement.

MO CHI:

Would you like to read it first, my father-in-law?

CHIN SUNG:

You read it first.

MO CHI:

Would you like to read it first, Yü Nu?

YU NU:

No, you read it first.

MO CHI:

Let's read together, then.

Reads

This is to announce the appointment of Sir Mo Chi to the rank of Chin-shih, eighth order.

Mo Chi *laughs heartily.*

CHIN SUNG:

What is it?

MO CHI:

I passed! Paste the announcement on the door!

Hands the announcement to the Messenger.

MESSENGER:

Yes, my lord.

Messenger *pastes the paper on the imaginary door.*

MESSENGER:

To Chin Sung

Ask the gentleman to give me a tip.

CHIN SUNG:

Tip? Oh, yes, a tip, of course.

Searches his pocket and finds himself penniless. Apologetically he gives the bowl to the messenger.

Here–here's a little something for you.

MESSENGER:

Looks disgustedly at Chin Sung.

Who wants your cold rice?

Messenger *exits to the right and* Chin Sung *comes back to* Mo Chi.

CHIN SUNG:

Hurry! My son-in-law has passed. He is now a Chin-shih, and that makes me a Chin-shih's father-in-law.

Dances proudly around the stage.

MO CHI:

Yes, I'm a high official now.

Seriously and sternly.

From now on, there must be strict discipline around here. I don't want to see any monkey business from you any more.

YU NU:

Motions to Chin Sung *to go out of the temple and whispers.*

Father, did you hear that? You must be careful now. I don't want to see you suffer in your old age. You'd better be patient and stay with us.

MO CHI:

To himself, in the temple.

Ugh! How can I, a high official, have a beggar for a father-in-law and a beggar's daughter for a wife!

With the fire of murder in his eyes.

They must go! They must vanish!

Enter Messenger *again from right.*

MESSENGER:

News. Good news.

CHIN SUNG:

Angrily.

What?

MESSENGER:

Here is another announcement for Lord Mo Chi.

CHIN SUNG:

Angrily.

Wait here.

MESSENGER:

Yes, yes.

Chin Sung *and* Yü Nu *gesture to enter the temple.*

CHIN SUNG:

Humbly.

My son-in-law, there is a messenger waiting outside with another announcement.

MO CHI:

Order him to come in.

CHIN SUNG:

Yes, Sir.

Goes out of the temple.

CHIN SUNG:

To Messenger

Come on in. But be careful, the lord has changed his temper.

They go into the temple.

MESSENGER:

Salutations to your lordship.

He kowtows, then presents the announcement to Mo Chi. Chin Sung *and* Yü Nu *congregate around* Mo Chi *and try to read it.* Mo Chi *stares at them sternly. They retreat.* Mo Chi *reads the announcement alone.*

MO CHI:

Reads.

This is to announce the appointment of Sir Mo Chi as the magistrate of Teh-hua county.

Laughs. To Chin Sung.

Paste the announcement on the door.

CHIN SUNG:

Yes, sir.

Chin Sung *goes out of the temple with the announcement.* Messenger *follows.* Chin Sung *pastes the announcement on the wall.* Messenger *pulls his sleeve.*

CHIN SUNG:

Angrily

What now?

MESSENGER:

This time you should give me some tip.

CHIN SUNG:

Oh, of course.

Gives Messenger *the bowl.*

Take this and go to hell.

MESSENGER:

To himself.

I think I've met the devil today.

Throws the bowl off stage, exits through right.

Enter from the right a minor Official with four Lung T'ao *carrying fine clothes.*

OFFICIAL:

Is anyone there?

CHIN SUNG:

Who's there?

OFFICIAL:

We have come to help Lord Mo Chi assume his new post.

CHIN SUNG:

Just wait a minute.

Goes back to Mo Chi.

Sir, there is an official with four attendants here to take you to your new post.

MO CHI:

Order him to come in.

CHIN SUNG:

Yes, sir.

To the official

Be careful, the master is not in a good mood.

OFFICIAL:

Salutations to you, Lord Mo.

Kowtows.

MO CHI:

Arise!

OFFICIAL:

We brought two hundred taels of silver for you.

Gives him the bag.

MO CHI:

Wonderful!

CHIN SUNG:

Let me accept it for you.

Takes the bag.

MO CHI:

Now let me change into these fine clothes.

Accepts the fine clothes from one of the four Lung T'ao *who helps* Mo Chi *change as he turns his back to the audience.* Yü Nu *changes hers at the same time.*

OFFICIAL:

What about you, old man?

CHIN SUNG:

I am not used to fine clothes, I think I'd better have this one.

Picks out a servant's black gown.

OFFICIAL:

So you are only a servant?

CHIN SUNG:

No, I'm the father-in-law of Lord Mo.

OFFICIAL:

My apologies, honorable sir.

Helps him dress and gives him a hat to match the gown.

Shall I throw the old hat away?

CHIN SUNG:

No, no, I'd better keep the old hat in case he changes his mind about taking care of me.

Puts his old hat in his pocket and watches while Yü Nu *is helped into a red-silk embroidered knee-length jacket.*

CHIN SUNG:

All dressed up in elegant silk gown and hat, turns to the Official.

Give orders to open the way for the master . . .

All leave to the left.

SCENE FIVE

A few hours later on the same day. About 8 p.m. Beside the wide Yangtze River. Enter oarsman, from right. Flourish. Enter from the right four Lung T'ao, *who lead the way for* Mo Chi, Yü Nu, *and* Chin Sung, *all dressed in their new finery.* Yü Nu *starts to get into the imaginary boat first, but is shoved aside by* Mo Chi. *She is in such a rage she tries to jump into the river.* Chin Sung *pulls her back and helps her into the boat. The* Lung T'ao *exit to the left. Father and daughter weep.*

MO CHI:

Sits down on the left of the table, Yü Nu *on the right, while* Chin Sung *is left standing on the left like a servant.*

Order them to sail.

OARSMAN:

Yes, my lord, but the wind is too wild and the waves are too rough to set sail at this moment.

MO CHI:

We shall anchor here for the present, then.

OARSMAN:

Yes, my lord.

Oarsman *exits left.*

MO CHI:

Old Chin! Old Chin!

Yu Nu in her finery watches her servant girl beat Mo Chi, her husband-for-the-second-time.

CHIN SUNG:

Who is Old Chin?

Yü Nu *points to* Chin Sung. *He understands.*

Yes, my lord.

MO CHI:

Serve the wine.

CHIN SUNG:

Yes, sir.

Pours wine for Mo Chi *and* Yü Nu.

MO CHI:

My wife, please.

Offers Yü Nu *a cup. Sings.*

I have devoted my time to study
Since I was very young.
Fortune has cast
Favor upon me at last.
I have become famous and happy.

YU NU:

Husband and wife, on the deck,
Are enjoying their drink.
Here's wishing you all the luck
To get promotion and advancement.

Yü Nu *toasts to* Mo Chi, *then falls asleep, leaning on the table.*

MO CHI:

Old Chin, you may finish the leftovers outside.

CHIN SUNG:

Walking to the right, to the edge of the imaginary boat, with the wine pot and cups. Says to himself:

You dirty rogue, you bastard, you! I've saved you from hunger and cold at my doorstep. If it had not been for my daughter and me, where would you be now? You are a high official—thanks to us. Ugh, if you go on like this, treating me like a dog, I'd be no man if I didn't make you vomit out my soybean soup that saved your life. Oh, how miserable!

Falls down, intoxicated.

MO CHI:

Calling

Old Chin! Old Chin!

Realizes that he is already drunk.

Ai-ya! I heard everything Old Chin just said. If I mistreat him after I assume my new post, he will disclose everything about my past and it will ruin my future.

Meditates

Let me think. What shall I do? I know–I'll tempt his daughter to the edge of the boat, then I can easily push her into the river ...

CHIN SUNG:

Talking in his sleep.

Conscience . . .

MO CHI:

Old Chin, Old Chin. Who cares about conscience? I'll push her into the river and save my future. My wife, wake up!

Shakes Yü Nu.

YU NU:

Sleepily

What is it, my lord.

MO CHI:

There's a very bright moon tonight. How picturesque it looks, reflected in the river. Let's go out on deck to appreciate its beauty.

YU NU:

It's very windy out there. Let's not go.

MO CHI:

Oh, are you afraid of a little wind? Now, now, let me help you onto deck.

Tenderly and affectionately supporting Yü Nu.

YU NU:

Thank you, my lord, I will keep you company, then.

Both go to the edge of the boat, left.

MO CHI:

My lady, look far beyond!
Look at the river swiftly flowing,
And the moon brilliantly shining,
Casting its reflection on the water
Like a bright and sparkling mirror!
O, look, look, look!
Beyond is a carp, a carp with golden scales!

YU NU:

Where is it? Where is the carp with golden scales?

MO CHI:

There—over there!

Mo Chi *pushes* Yü Nu *into the river.*

YU NU:

Ai . . . ya!

River God *with four attendants holding banners painted with waves and fish to denote it is underwater, enters right. Brings* Yu Nu *to the left. They exit together upstage left.*

MO CHI:

Goes over to Chin Sung.

Old Chin, wake up!

CHIN SUNG:

Rises

What is the matter?

MO CHI:

Your daughter accidentally fell into the river.

CHIN SUNG:

Hey, oarsman, help–help and drag her out of the river.

Oarsman *rushes in.*

OARSMAN:

The water is so rapid that it must have already brought her down into the depths of the river. It's impossible to get her out now.

CHIN SUNG:

Ai-ya! My poor child!

Weeps

MO CHI:

Old Chin, you needn't cry. Here are twenty taels of silver.
Take this home with you and live in peace.

CHIN SUNG:

My dear son-in-law, she was the only daughter I had. Now she is dead and I have no one. I am all alone in the world, with no place to rest my bones. I beg you, let me stay with you. You don't have to treat me like a father-in-law–just treat me like one of your servants. Just give me leftovers from your table–a tiny bit of boiled rice will be good enough for me. Please–please let me go along with you!

MO CHI:

You don't know anything about the customs and manners of official life.

CHIN SUNG:

Although the customs and manners may be many, I can learn–a few each day. Perhaps after a year, I will be able to learn most of them. Besides, I was once the Chief of Beggars, so I know some of the manners of a court. If you take me along with you, you don't even have to treat me like a human being. Just treat me like a dog or a cat. Oh, I beseech you to take care of me in my old age.

Begging on his knees.

MO CHI:

How annoying!

Turns his back on Chin Sung.

CHIN SUNG:

Rising

You ungrateful, cold-blooded Mo Chi! Don't you have any regard for the ones who saved your life? If it hadn't been for us, how could you have seen this day of fortune? I have begged you to let me stay with you, but you are so hardhearted that my pleadings haven't even touched you. Here, I don't want to have any of your things!

Takes off the silk gown and hat and throws them on the deck, and takes his old hat from his pocket.

I knew I'd need my old hat one of these days!

Puts on the old beggar's hat.

MO CHI:

Kick him off the boat, oarsman!

CHIN SUNG:

There's no need. I can go ashore myself.

Jumps out of the boat to front stage.

Mo Chi, Mo Chi, you cunning, ungrateful rogue! If heaven has eyes, you will be punished. Then I will surely make you vomit my soybean soup out of your damned bastard head.

Picks up an imaginany stone and throws it at the boat.

I'll kill you! I will!

MO CHI:

Oarsman, hurry up and set sail.

Chin Sung *continues to throw stones.*

SCENE SIX

The place of action is now Lin Jun's boat sailing on the river as indicated by the oarsman. Yü Nu *enters and lies as if dead downstage right. Enter four guards, two oarsmen, two maids, a servant followed by* Lin Jun *and* Madam Lin.

LIN JUN:

Sings

The boat is sailing in rough weather today.

MADAM LIN:

Sings

The river has been misty and blurry for days.

They sit, Lin Jun *on the left of the table and* Madam Lin *on the right.*

OARSMAN A:

My lord, the wind is too fierce to sail any farther.

LIN JUN:

Anchor the boat then.

OARSMAN B:

O, look, there is a corpse in the river.

Pointing at Yü Nu

LIN JUN:

Make haste and drag it out.

The oarsmen bring Yu Nu *to the imaginary boat.*

LIN JUN:

See if she is still alive.

OARSMAN A:

She breathes, she still breathes.

LIN JUN:

Give her some sweet ginger soup.

The servant *brings a bowl for* Yu Nu.

YU NU:

Wakes up and sings.

I hear voices pounding in my ears. But now what do I see? Maids and attendants all standing in a row!

Stands up

Oh, where am I?

SERVANT:

Our master, Lord Lin, has saved your life. Why don't you come forward and thank him for his kindness?

YU NU:

Goes to Lin Jun *and kowtows*

I am extremely grateful to you, Lord Lin, for saving my life.

LIN JUN:

Get up and sit down please.

Yu Nu *gets up and sits on the right beside* Madam Lin.

LIN JUN:

My girl, what is your name and how did you fall into the river?

YU NU:

Since you are my savior, I'll tell you.

Sings

I am Chin Yu Nu, the only daughter of the Chief of Beggars, Chin Sung. My mother died when I was very young, so my father has been both Father and Mother to me and has loved me very dearly. A few months ago, Mo Chi, who was poor and homeless but a *hsiu-tsai,* came along. Since he was suffering from cold and starvation, my father took pity on him and since he was learned and promising, my father asked me to marry him. We were all very happy and I encouraged him to take the government advanced examination. He was fortunate to pass it and was appointed magistrate of Teh-Hua County. My father and I set sail with him for his new post . . . But how could I have thought that he was so cold-blooded as to push me into the river. Lord Lin, if you hadn't saved me I would have been drowned.

Weeps

Ah, ya, my lord! I have no one to blame but my own fate.

LIN JUN:

Sings

Oh, I can't stand such ingratitude! It makes me so furious that my hair seems to shoot up three thousand feet away.

MADAM LIN:

Sings

That Mo Chi is cruel indeed.

LIN JUN:

Now where is your father?

YU NU:

He came with us on the same boat, but I don't know where he is now.

LIN JUN:

Poor girl! I am Lin Jun, the new governor of Kiangsi and your husband, the magistrate of Tẹh Hua, is one of my subordinates. Since we have no children of our own, we intend to adopt you as our daughter. Meanwhile I will try my best to look for your father and husband. What do you think of my idea?

YU NU:

Very happy to be the adopted daughter of Lin, *stands up and kowtows before* Lin Jun *and* Madam Lin.

Papa and Mama, please accept my humble greetings.

Remains kneeling and turns, facing the audience.

Oh, God of the Boat, I hereby vow that from this day on I will be pious to Lord Lin and Madam Lin as to my own parents if they were alive.

LIN JUN:

Maids, take Miss into the inner cabins and change her wet clothes.

YU NU:

Thank you very much, Papa and Mama.

Stands up and walks upstage toward the right.

Softly.

I am going to the inner cabins to change my clothes. Ai-ya, when shall I see my ungrateful husband again?

Exit Yü Nu *with a maid by the right door.*

LIN JUN:

Servant, come here.

Servant *answers "aye".*

LIN JUN:

Take a suit of fine clothes, go down the street and look for Mr. Chin Sung, my adopted daughter's father. As soon as you find him, ask him to change his clothes and bring him back with you. Hurry and no delay.

SERVANT:

Yes, my lord, I'll go right away.

Exit Servant *to the right.*

LIN JUN:

Oarsmen, when Mr. Chin comes, report to me immediately. Madam, let us go in and rest a while.

They all go out by the left door.

SCENE SEVEN

A month later. An afternoon in October.
Chin Sung *enters right.*

CHIN SUNG:

If there ever was an ungrateful creature, it is that Mo Chi! He forced me out of the boat and left me to starve. It's a good thing begging is my profession. Now, at last, I am in Kiangsi.

Yawns.

Another day is over. I must find a place to rest my tired old bones.

Starts toward left and accidentally bumps into one of Governor Lin's *servants who is coming out of the upstage left door with a bundle in his hand.*

Hey you, are you blind? How dare you bump me! I, Chin Sung, would swat you if I had the energy!

Continues on his way.

SERVANT:

Hey, come back here! Did you say Chin Sung?

CHIN SUNG:

What if I did?

SERVANT:

And do you have a daughter named Yü Nu?

CHIN SUNG:

Yes, I did, but she is now dead and gone.

Starts to go away, his shoulders drooping.

SERVANT:

Please come back, Mr. Chin!

CHIN SUNG:

Who is Mr. Chin?

SERVANT:

It's you, Mr. Chin. Your daughter, Yü Nu, was saved from drowning by my master, Lin Jun, the Governor of Kiangsi, and now she's become his adopted daughter. Governor Lin has ordered me to look for you with these fine clothes so that I can take you home to live with your daughter.

CHIN SUNG:

Is it true? Oh, Heaven has eyes indeed! Where are the fine clothes? Help me put them on.

SERVANT:

Here they are.

Helps Chin Sung *change clothes.*

CHIN SUNG:

Now I don't need this old hat any more.

Throws it away and puts on a fancy hat to match his elaborate gown.

Lead the way, servant! Lead the way for Mr. Chin!

They both exit left.

SCENE EIGHT

Enter four attendants, servant, and then Lin Jun *from right.*
Lin Jun, *the Governor of Kiangsi, is seated in the center, with an empty chair at his right. Four attendants are dressed in elaborate gowns, two on each side.* Lin Jun *wears a blue-silk gown and shining headdress.*

LIN JUN:
Order the magistrate from Teh Hua to come in.

BUTLER:
Calls, facing the left door.
Come in Magistrate from Teh Hua.
Enter Mo Chi *who is now the magistrate of Teh Hua.*

MO CHI:
Salutations to your Excellency.

LIN JUN:
To Mo Chi.
Please be seated.

MO CHI:
How dare I sit before Your Excellency?

LIN JUN:
I want to talk things over informally with you, so please relax.

MO CHI:
Thank you, Your Excellency.
Sits on the right chair.

LIN JUN:
So you are Magistrate Mo Chi! Let me ask you, have you brought your wife along with you to your new post?

MO CHI:

I did, but she accidentally fell into the river and was drowned.

LIN JUN:

Ah, too bad. But it just so happens that I have a daughter, whom I want you to marry.

MO CHI:

Pleased but embarrassed.

But . . .

LIN JUN:

How do you like to be my son-in-law?

MO CHI:

My humble salutations to you, my honorable father-in-law.

Kneels.

LIN JUN:

Today is the lucky day, Mo Chi—prepare for the wedding ceremony.

They all rise. Music. Exit all to the right.

SCENE NINE

The back of the stage now represents the bridal chamber. In the center is hung a pair of closed curtains, behind which a chair is placed for the bride. Yü Nu *sings* Hsi-P'i-Tao-Pan *from behind the upstage right door, Enter from the right* Yü Nu *with a red silk handkerchief to cover her head and face and dressed in red, attended by two maids. She sings* Hsi-P'i-Man-Pan *while walking around the stage.*

YU NU:

I never expected to be a bride a second time, and to the same bridegroom!

To the maids.

Have you got the clubs and sticks ready? Beat that cold-blooded man as hard as you can!

Sits down and the maids let down the curtains on either side. The two maids stands, with clubs and sticks ready, in the center. Enter an elated Mo Chi, *from the right.*

MO CHI:

Laughing.

I'm so glad that the beggar's daughter is dead. Now I am married for the second time, and to a girl from a rich and respectable family. This is a great day for me!

MAID A:

Let's get ready to beat him up!

MO CHI:

Ah . . why are you holding sticks and clubs . . . and at the door of the bridal chamber?

MAID B:

Are you Mo Chi, the bridegroom?

MO CHI:

Exactly.

MAID A:

Do you know our wedding custom here?

MO CHI:

No, I don't.

MAID B:

Then, let us tell you. Before you enter the bridal chamber, you must receive forty strokes from our clubs and sticks.

MO CHI:

What a funny custom!

MAID A:

No more talk. Let's beat him up.

Starts beating Mo Chi.

MO CHI:

Ouch! Hey, not so hard! Have mercy! Help! Ouch!

YU NU:

Girls, enough now. Make him come in humbly, with his head bowed.

MAID A:

By order of our young mistress, you are to bow your head as you go in.

MO CHI:

Yes, yes, yes!

Steps over the doorsill into the bridal chamber.

YU NU:

Kneel down and face the door.

MO CHI:

Yes, your ladyship.

Kneels with his face toward the audience. His back is toward Yü Nu, *who reveals herself when the curtains are drawn apart by the maids.*

YU NU:

Tell me, did you have a wife?

MO CHI:

Yes, I did, but she accidentally fell off a boat and was drowned.

YU NU:

Oh, how tragic! So she fell into the river and drowned, eh? Turn your head around and look at me, and see if I am prettier than your former wife.

MO CHI:

Oh, how I have longed for the day to feast my eyes on your beautiful face!

Turns around and sees Yü Nu. *Jumps up in fright.*

Oh, help! A ghost! a ghost!

YU NU:

Girls, beat him up again.

The maids strike Mo Chi.

MO CHI:

Ouch! Help! O, have mercy on me!

YU NU:

All right, girls, you can stop now.

The girls stand aside.

Be seated, you cruel man.

Mo Chi *sits with great difficulty.*

Don't you remember how hungry and cold you were when you fainted on our doorsteps? It was I who gave you some hot soybean soup to save your life. My father made me your wife, hoping that he could be taken care of when he became old. How happy we were in the early days of our marriage! You were so well-fed and clothed that you forgot about your ambitions and wanted to enjoy life and leisure for the rest of your days. It was I who inspired you to take the government examinations.

It was my father who begged for your food and your way to the capital for the examinations. Fate smiled on you when you passed with the *chin shih* degree, 8th rank. You were not too bad when the good news of your success first came, but when it came the second time, you became so snobbish that you treated my father worse than a cheap slave. Where was your sense of mercy and righteousness then?

On our way to your new post, you realized that I was the daughter of the Chief of Beggars that would ruin your future, so you tempted me to go on deck and pushed me, pushed me into the bottom of the river.

Thanks to my adopted father, Lord Lin, I was saved from drowning. When he learned about your cold-bloodedness, he was very angry and wanted to go to the capital at once to report you to the authorities. You would have been dismissed from your important post if I had not begged and begged him not to do so. Look at you, all dressed up in fineries like a gentleman. You are nothing but a hypocrite!

Points a shaking finger at Mo Chi.

Ungrateful rogue, how do you have the nerve to face me again!

To the maids.

Beat him . . . chase him out of my sight. How I hate him!

MO CHI:

O, my wife! Can't we let bygones be bygones? Forgive me! From now on, I will look on you with deep respect. I beg you for mercy!

YU NU:

Nothing doing! It isn't that easy. You can promise everything one minute and forget all about it the next.

The maids *strike him away from the bridal chamber.*

Enter Chin Sung *from the right.*

CHIN SUNG:

Who says there isn't justice in this world? Ah, now I am content. Let me take a look at the fun in the bridal chamber.

Walking toward Mo Chi, *who blocks his way.*

Only a stray dog blocks the way. Let's see who this is.

Bends to look at Mo Chi.

MO CHI:

Looking up pathetically.

My honorable father-in-law.

CHIN SUNG:

So it's you, ungrateful dog! This is your reward for being a cruel, cold-blooded murderer! You didn't want us around when we were poor, did you? Heaven is just. Now you are at my mercy. I must beat you hard before I can really be happy again.

Takes a stick from a maid to strike Mo Chi, Mo Chi *rises to escape the blows but bumps into* Lin Jun, *who at this very moment enters from the right.* Mo Chi *kowtows.*

LIN JUN:

How dare you? You shameless Mo Chi! You call yourself educated and a scholar, and yet you have done such terrible things! I will report you to the Emperor and have your title taken away. You'll be dismissed from your post!

YU NU:

Goes over to Lin *and kowtows.*

Ah, dear adopted father, for my sake, please pardon him!

LIN JUN:

Only for your sake will I pardon him.

Seeing Chin Sung.

Ah, my matrimonial ally.

CHIN SUNG:

Yes, my benefactor?

LIN JUN:

For your daughter's sake, you'd better pardon him, too.

CHIN SUNG:

As you please, my benefactor.

LIN JUN:

All right, let's pardon him. Still . . . his heartless cruelty is dreadful!

YU NU:

How could he have pushed me in the river?

MO CHI:

Getting to his feet.

Let's forget about the past, dear. We should be happy and thankful now that we can have a grand family reunion.

LIN JUN:

Yes, let's forget the evil and remember only virtue. Now, let's all go and enjoy the wedding feast.

CHIN SUNG:

Once a father-in-law, always a father-in-law!

All go off stage to the left. Curtair

ONE MISSING HEAD

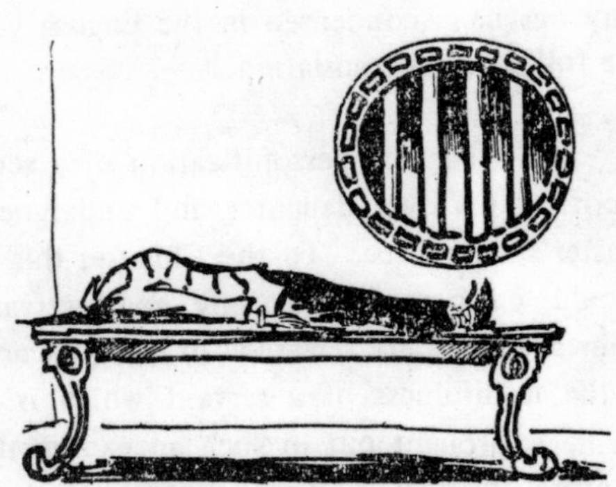

(Chiu Keng T'ien)

This story is a bit grisly to modern Western eyes, but the Chinese have loved it for centuries. *One Missing Head* affords an opportunity for the *lao sheng* to show his skill in singing and acting. It somewhat resembles the blood-and-thunder tragedy of the English First Elizabethan period, with its violence, bloodshed, ghosts, and eventual justice.

The Chinese title, *Chiu Keng T'ien* (九更天), literally means "The Night of Nine Strokes." The opera is adapted from a story, written about the end of the Ming dynasty, which was called "The Mystery of the Delayed Dawn." A faithful servant, Ma Yi, saves his master's life by appealing to the Grand Tutor the night before the dawn that the execution is to take place. To announce the passage of a two-hour interval, the night watchmen usually begin to strike the gong at nine o'clock with one stroke until dawn with five strokes at five o'clock. On this night the gods take pity on the accused: the watchmen have to strike their gongs nine times, instead of the usual five. Because the night has been magically prolonged, Ma Yi is given the opportunity to plead for his master, and the Grand Tutor has time to go to the county seat to stay the execution.

Because there are a considerable number of short scenes in *Chiu Keng T'ien* which merely lend authenticity to the Chinese title, this nonessential aspect of the play has been condensed in the English version. Otherwise, *One Missing Head* is the full story in translation.

Ma Yi is the personification of a servant's fidelity to his master. He even sacrifices his own daughter and undergoes various painful tortures to prove his master's innocence. To the Chinese, this trait of pure fidelity is admirable and should be possessed by any good servant. Although many other traditional Chinese virtues are rewarded in this play and the lack of them punished severely, it is the faithfulness of a servant which is the predominant theme. In fact, this theme is brought out in such an exaggerated fashion that perhaps one can only interpret the play as satire, a savagely satirical attack on precisely that virtue.

This play was produced in English for the first time outside China at the University of North Carolina at Greensboro on May 10, 1967, while I was a Fulbright professor there. I added six more scenes to the six scenes in the version in the edition in *Children of the Pear Garden* in order to lend authenticity to the Chinese title, *Chiu Keng T'ien,* or *The Night of the Nine Strokes,* and to show that justice is always upheld in China. Co-directed by Professor Kathryn England and me, it enjoyed great success and received excellent reviews from the drama critics in Greensboro and the neighboring cities.

"Any reservations that the Wednesday opening night audience might have had about the Chinese opera *One Missing Head* were quickly and permanently erased. . . . What struck me immediately about this play was its great likeness to Shakes peare's tragedies. It was profuse with vile thoughts and bloody deeds. And there were plenty of ghosts and witches to top it off."–Jim McAllister, Daily News Entertainment Editor, *Greensboro Daily News,* May 11, 1967.

"*One Missing Head* has all the ingredients of good theatre–and interesting, if somewhat gruesome, plot, capable actors, beautiful costumes and music that contributes to the mood of the play." –Dorothy Benjamin, Record Staff Writer, Greensboro Record, May 12, 1967.

ONE MISSING HEAD

Characters

MI CHIN-T'U . . . . *a young scholar*
(米 進 圖)

MA YI . . . . *faithful servant to Mi Chin-T'u*
(馬 義)

MISTRESS YAO . . . . *sister-in-law to Mi Chin-T'u*
(姚 氏)

HOU HUA-TSUI . . . . *paramour of Mistress Yao*
(侯 花 嘴)

MISTRESS LI . . . . *wife of Hou Hua-Tsui*
(李 氏)

MAGISTRATE . . . . *magistrate of Mo Li County*
(米進卿魂)

MAMA MA . . . . *wife of Ma Yi*
(馬 媽 媽)

MA YUEH-HSIANG . . . . *daughter of Ma Yi*
(馬 月 香)

GRAND TUTOR WEN of the Imperial Court

THE GHOST OF MI CHIN-CH'ING, brother to Chin-T'u

WATCHMEN, GUARDS

SCENE ONE

The scene is a room at an inn. Early morning. A chair is placed in front of a table in the center of the stage. Enter Mi Chin-T'u from upstage right. Mi, a young man of about twenty-six, has a long flowing, light blue gown with floral designs, kimona style, with a soft hat to match. He walks downstage center.

MI CHIN-T'U:

I am full of precious education. But when will I achieve success and reputation?

Turns counter clockwise, walks to the chair and sits down.

I, Mi Chin-T'u am a young scholar. *Raises both hands, the knuckles of one clasped with the other.* My parents died when I was very young. My older brother, Mi Chin-Ch'ing, took good care of me, brought me up and gave me a fine education. By the order of my brother and sister-in-law, I am to take the State Civil Service Examination. I am now on my way to the capital with my faithful servant, Ma Yi, to find my fortune. Last night we stopped at this little inn. In the middle of the night I had a horrible dream. I dreamed that my brother, all bleeding, came to me, clamoring for revenge. I am very much upset, I can't figure out what it meant. I'd better call Ma Yi out and ask him. Ma Yi, where are you?

MA YI:

Off stage

Coming!

Enter Ma Yi from upstage right. He wears a long black gown with an orange sash, and a black cap. He is an old man of about fiftyfive. He walks downstage center.

I heard my master call me. I wonder what he wants. Let me go to him quickly.

He gestures to cross the threshold to enter the room and bows before Mi Chin-T'u.

Greetings to Second Master!

He goes and stands to left.

What can I do for you, Second Master?

CHIN-T'U:

Last night I dreamed that my brother came to my room. He was bleeding all over his body and he asked me to avenge the wrong done to him. I can't understand this frightening dream.

MA YI:

I had the same horrible dream, too. This is an evil omen.
We'd better go home and find out.

CHIN-T'U:

Right you are. Let's check out of this inn and go on our way.

MA YI:

Yes, Second Master.

Walking toward the right and turning toward upstage.

Innkeeper!

IMMKEEPER:

Off stage.

What do you want?

MA YI:

We are leaving. We have paid for our night's lodging here on the desk.

INNKEEPER:

Off stage

Thank you. Please come again. Good-bye.

MA YI:

Yes, my master.

CHIN-T'U:

Getting up

Bring my horse.

Ma Yi crosses stage to go to the table upstage as Property Man enters from upstage left with a tasseled stick and a red bundle and walks to the table.

Ma Yi *puts the red bundle over his left shoulder, takes the tasseled stick to represent the horse from the prop man walks downstage center and holds it for* Chin-T'u *to mount.* Mi *sings "hsi p'i yao pan."*

Ma Yi *and* Mi Chin-T'u exit to upstage left.

SCENE TWO

The sitting room of the Mi *family.*

There are curtains at the back. In the center of the stage is a table with two chairs on either side.

It is early evening.

MISTRESS YAO is seen walking in from upstage right. She is about 25, has a red knee-length jacket with a white collar, white undersleeves, and a long pleated skirt. She wears a large white flower on her head to indicate she is in mourning. She appears restless and worried.

MISTRESS YAO:

I am Mistress Yao.

I've been trembling and my heart jumps every time I hear the slightest sound since the death of my husband. What if my brother-in-law comes back and discovers the truth?

She sings hsi p'i yao pan *as* Mi Chin-T'u *and* Ma Yi *enter from upstage right and walk to downstage right.* Mi *hands the horse to* Ma *and goes to downstage center to knock on the imaginary door.*

Who is it?

She shivers nervously.

Just a minute!

She takes off her red jacket, revealing a white one to denote she is in mourning.

YAO quickly hides the red jacket under the table, comes to downstage center and gestures to open the imaginary door. Enter Ma Yi and Mi Chin-T'u.

CHIN-T'U:

Yes, I'm back.

Surprised.

How are you, sister-in-law?

YAO:

Fine. Please come in, fine, ah . . . sit down, please.

They sit, Chin-T'u *on the left and* Yao *on the right.*

MA YI:

Bows.

My salutations to you, madam.

YAO:

You must have had a long trip, you'd better go in and rest.

MA YI:

Thank you, Madam.

Exit to upstage left.

CHIN-T'U:

Why are you in mourning, my sister-in-law?

YAO:

Oh, it's for your brother.

Chin-T'u *is surprised and jumps up.*

Pretends to weep.

You see, since you left, he missed you so much that he became sick and died!

CHIN-T'U:

Jumps up. Yao *also jumps up and looks at him tremblingly.*

Mi *goes downstage left and goes the tou-hsiu with his right sleeve.*

Oh, poor brother! No wonder both Ma Yi and I had the same terrible dream.

I saw my brother come bleeding to me, clamoring for revenge.

At the word revenge, Yao *becomes pale and trembles, but* Chin-t'u *is too sad to notice.*

Oh, my brother, my brother, how could you leave us?

Goes to Yao.

Where is his coffin?

YAO:

Points to downstage left

In the study.

CHIN-T'u:

I want to pay my respects to his soul before his coffin.

YAO:

Weeps.

Pointing to the left.

This way, please.

Weeps.

Yao *and* Chin-t'u *come to the front stage left and lift their feet to indicate passing across the threshold to enter another room, as the Propman moves a table with white covering to downstage left.*

CHIN-T'U:

Kneels before a table just placed by the Property Man. The table is covered with a little white cloth on top to represent the coffin.

Ah, my brother Chin-ch'ing. Brother Chin-ch'ing! I cannot but shed tears before your spirit. Ah, Brother Chin-ch'ing! It's like a sharp knife thrusting into my heart when I think of you lying motionless and silent, enclosed in the cold, cold coffin! Can you hear me, my brother?

Cries and knowtows before the table.

YAO:

Brother-in-law, since your brother is now dead, oceans of tears will not make him come back to life again. So cry no more.

CHIN-T'U:

Stands up.

Sister-in-law, I want to stay up all night to watch his coffin.

YAO:

You will surely be lonely all by yourself. Let me keep you company.

CHIN-T'U:

Now that my brother is dead, people will gossip if you keep me company all night.

YAO:

To right.

Who cares? We belong to the same family, don't we?

Coquettishly.

Let me keep you company . . . please?

Approaches him flirtatiously, and puts both of her sleeves on Mi's *left shoulder.*

CHIN-T'U:

Jumps up.

Ugh! What propriety is this? Outrageous!

He shows disgust and exits to upstage left.

YAO:

Ah, Chin-t'u, you ungrateful fool! No regard for my kindness, eh! And insulting me, too. All right . . . I'll get even with you . . . I'll go and talk it over with Monkey Flower Mouth.

Points assuringly to the andience goes to put on the red jacket and exit to upstage right.

SCENE THREE

The scene is now in the house of MONKEY FLOWER MOUTH, Yao's paramour.

At the back is a pair of closed curtains in front of a chair, to indicate the bedroom.

On the left is a table with two chairs on either side.

Two cups and a wine pot are on the table. Enter Monkey Flower Mouth from upstage left and Yao *from upstage right. Hou's name,* Hua-tsui, *means "flower-mouth," while his surname,* Hou, *is almost similar to the Chinese word for "Monkey," and is pronounced the same. This name pun is rather important to the plot of this simple folk story.* Hou Hua-tsui *is about 35, with a rather large red mouth, and somewhat resembles a monkey.*

MONKEY FLOWER MOUTH:

Opens the door, steps out.

Oh, it's you.

Yao gestures to come in. Monkey follows and closes the door.

Why are you so late tonight? Ah, I see my darling little widow can't stand the loneliness. She needs me, doesn't she?

Pinches her cheek.

YAO:

That terrible Chin-t'u is back and I'm afraid he'll discover that *we've* killed his brother. You must think of a way to put us out of danger!

PLONKEY:

Thinks for a moment.

Here's a wonderful idea! Let me make my wife drunk and then have her killed. Chop off her head and put her into your clothes. Drag her to your door, then report to the police, saying Chin-t'u tried to seduce you, a poor widow. Being refused, he chops off your head. We can be rid of him quickly. See what a genius I am?

YAO:

You are a dear, wonderful man! It's a great scheme!

MONKEY:

But you must help me do it.

YAO:

All right, but don't let a soul in on our secret.

Exits to upstage left.

MONKEY:

Calling to the right.

Hey, wife, come out!

Enter from upstage right Mistress Li, a very ugly woman of 35, plump and square-faced.

MISTRESS LI:

Yes, my master.

MONKEY:

Please be seated.

They both sit, Monkey *on the left and his wife on the right.*

My dear wife, I have decided to be a good husband from now on and I promise not to look at another woman! I'll stay with you forever. Here is some delicious food and wine for a celebration. Let's have a party!

Pours wine into two cups and gives one to his wife.

LI:

Very pleased.

I knew you would come back to me! Oh, thank you!

Drinks deeply.

MONKEY:

How do you feel now?

LI:

Oh, I feel dizzy. I think I'm already drunk!

Giggles crazily.

MONKEY:

Let me help you to bed.

Supports Li *to the closed curtains in front of the imaginary bedroom.*

LI:

Behind the curtains.

Oh, come to bed with me, I'm lonely!

MONKEY:

Coming, coming!

Walks to the left, claps his hands.

Mistress Yao *tiptoes in from upstage left.*

YAO:

What's going on?

MONKEY:

She's in there . . . drunk . . .

YAO:

Let me take a look at her.

Peeps behind the curtains.

Ai-ya! What an ugly woman! Where's the dagger?

MONKEY:

Takes a dagger from his sleeve.

Here it is.

YAO:

Kill her then!

MONKEY:

I don't know how. You do it.

YAO:

You do it.

MONKEY:

No, you do it.

YAO:

All right–let me do it.

Goes behind the curtains and returns with a wild look in her eyes and the bloody dagger.

Done! Now what?

ONKEY:

Now you take off your jacket and put it on her. Cut off her head and hide it under the bed.

Mistress Yao *disappears behind the curtains and the audience can hear the sound of a head being chopped off, the rustle of clothes, and a dragging sound.* Yao *appears with the corpse. She is now in* Li's *clothes.* Monkey *helps her drag the headless corpse off stage to upstage left (toward* Yao's *house). He reappears immediately; after a slight pause,* Yao *also reappears.*

YAO:

Now you'd better go and report it to the police. I'll wait for you here.

MONKEY:

Don't budge out of this room.

YAO:

I know. I know. Come back as soon as you can.

Exit Monkey *to the right and* Yao *gestures to close the door and exits to the left.*

SCENE FOUR

The scene is the street. Enter two guards of the court of the magistrate, dressed in black gowns with red sashes from upstage right. They walk to downstage center.

GUARDS:

We are the two guards of the magistrate's court of Mo Li County. Since there is neither a civil nor a criminal case today, we are taking a walk outside the courthouse.

Enter Monkey Flower-Mouth *from upstage right.*

MONKEY:

Greetings, guards!

GUARDS:

Oh, greetings, Mr. Monkey, why are you in such a hurry?

MONKEY:

Don't you know there was a murder committed in this county?

GUARDS:

Murder! What murder?

MONKEY:

Mi Chin-t'u tried to rape his widowed sister-in-law.
Failing so, he put an end to her sweet, young life.

GUARDS:

How do you know?

MOKEY:

Eh—Well, I saw . . I saw the dead body lying there at their back door. You see, their back door is across the street from my front door. That's how I know, yes, I saw it with my own eyes. That's how I know.

GUARDS:

Mr. Monkey, you go ahead and report this murder to the magistrate and we'll go and arrest Mi Chin-t'u.

MONKEY:

Yes, I was just going there when I met you. Good-bye.
Now, be sure to arrest Mi Chin-t'u.

Exit Monkey Flower-Mouth *to upstage left.*

GUARD A:

Let's go and catch Mi Chin-t'u before he gets away. Let's go.

They walk around the stage and stop downstage center.

GUARD B:

This must be the house of Mi.

Ma Yi appeals for justice to Grand Tutor Wen before he is tortured with the thirty-six heavenly nails.

GUARD A:

Gestures to knock at the imaginary door.

Open the door! Open the door!

Enter Ma Yi *from upstage left.*

MA YI:

I heard people talking and knocking at our door. Who is it?

Going downstage center, gesturing to open the door and stepping out of the house.

GUARD A:

Is Mi Chin-t'u in the house?

MA YI:

Yes, he is in, but why do you want to see him?

GUARD A:

Ask him to come out.

MA YI:

Turning toward upstage left.

Second Master, please come out.

Enter Mi Chin-t'u *from upstage left, walks to downstage center and steps out of the house.*

CHIN-T'U:

What is it?

MA YI:

There are two guards from the court. They want to see you.

GUARD A:

Are you Mi Chin-t'u?

CHIN-T'U:

Yes, I am.

GUARD B:

Putting the chains on Mi.

Come with us. You are under arrest.

MA YI:

Trying to stop the guards.

Why did you arrest my second master?

GUARDS:

If you want to know why, come to the court and find out.

Exit two guards with Mi Chin-t'u *to the left.*

MA YI:

Ah-ya! I just don't understand. My second master came back yesterday only to find my first master dead. He was so sad that he kept watch over the coffin all night. Now early this morning two guards came from the courthouse and arrested him. This is simply beyond my comprehension.

Pause.

Now I have got it. Let me go to the courthouse myself and find out what this is all about. Yes, that's the thing to do.

Exit Ma Yi *to upstage left.*

SCENE FIVE

The scene is now the court of the magistrate. The chair is placed behind the table to represent the courthouse. On the table are placed a block (the size of two shoeboxes, on top of each other) wrapped with a piece of yellow cloth to represent the official seal, an ink slab, paper and some writing brushes. Enter from the left four attendants, dressed in black gowns with blue trimmings and red sashes. They come two by two, walk to the center of stage, separate and stand on either side of the table, two on each side. Enter the Magistrate of Mo Li County. He is in royal blue formal official gown with a stiff hoop-like jade girdle and a black official gauze hat. He walks downstage center, turns clockwise and walks to the chair and sits down.

MAGISTRATE:

I am the Magistrate of Mo Li County. My job is to right all kinds of injustice.

Enter Monkey Flower-Mouth *from the right. He gestures to enter the court and kneels before the* Magistrate.

MONKEY:

Salutations to your Honor!

Gets up and stands on the left.

MAGISTRATE:

What is your grievance?

MONKEY:

I have no grievance. I am here to report to you a crime that was committed in your county.

MAGISTRATE:

What? A crime committed in my county?

MONKEY:

Yes, Mi Chin-t'u murdered his widowed sister-in-law just because she didn't want to be seduced.

MAGISTRATE:

Was his sister-in-law related to you?

MONKEY:

Oh, no, she didn't have any relation with me. No, not at all.

MAGISTRATE:

If she was not related to you nor did she have any relation with you, why did you make the report?

MONKEY:

Well—er—Since I found the corpse at their back door which is directly across the street from my front door, I'm afraid that people may suspect me of the crime.

MAGISTRATE:

All right, you may go now, But come back in three days to watch the trial.

MONKEY:

Kneeling.

Thank you, your honor.

Exit Monkey *to the right.*

Enter two guards with Chin-t'u *from upstage right.*

MAGISTRATE

Pretends to write on a parchment and hands it to a guard.

Take this warrant to arrest Mi Chin-t'u.

Guard A *gestures to enter the court and kneels before the* Magistrate.

GUARD A:

Your Honor, we have already caught Mi Chin-t'u.

MAGISTRATE:

Bring him in.

Guard A *gets up, goes out of the court and brings in* Mi Chin-t'u.

Ma Yi *enters quietly from the right and stands downstage right.*

CHIN-T'U:

Kneeling before the Magistrate.

Salutations to your Honor from the student, Mi Chin-t'u.

MAGISTRATE:

Mi Chin-t'u, since you are a student, you must be well-educated.

CHIN-T'U:

Yes, in a way I am, Your Honor. But I am only a Bachelor of Arts of the lowest rank.

MAGISTRATE:

So you are educated and learned—a student should be upright and righteous. How could you murder your widowed sister-in-law? Why did you kill her? Speak up and admit your crime!

CHIN-T'U:

How can I do such a horrible thing? Since I am a student, all I know is to study hard for the State Examination.

MAGISTRATE:

Guards, take him to the detention house until I return from my thorough investigation of this case. Take him out.

A guard leads Mi Chin-t'u *out to upstage left. Ma Yi watches, takes a step forward, lowers his head and quietly goes out to the right.*

Come, guards, lead the way to the site of the murder and let me examine the corpse.

All go out to upstage right.

SCENE SIX

The scene is now Monkey Flower-Mouth's *house. Enter* Monkey *from upstage right. He walks downstage.*

MONKEY:

My scheme is a total success and my work is done. Let me go back to my sweetie love.

He gestures to knock on the imaginary door downstage center.

Hey, open the door!

Mistress Yao *comes out from the left and gestures to open the door.*

YAO:

O, so you are back.

Monkey *looks around, gestures to come in and close the door.*

MONKEY:

Yes, yes, I am back.

YAO:

Tell me about your report to the magistrate.

MONKEY:

Everything was done just right. Aren't you proud of me?

YAO:

Yes, you're a genius . . .

Takes a few steps away and then coyly.

I think I'd better go home now since everything's settled.

MONKEY:

Just wait a moment. Aren't you supposed to be dead? How can you go home now?

YAO:

Then where am I going to stay?

MONKEY:

Why, here with me, of course. We've gotten rid of that fat ugly wife of mine and your dull husband. Now nobody is in our way. We can do whatever we like. Let's go to the back of the house and enjoy ourselves.

Exeunt Monkey *and* Yao *hand in hand to upstage left.*

SCENE SEVEN

The scene is the same as in Scene Five. Enter four attendants, followed by the Magistrate *from upstage right.*

MAGISTRATE:

Sitting.

Bring in Mi Chin-t'u.

Enter a guard with Mi Chin-t'u *from upstage left.* Mi Chin-t'u *kneels before the magistrate.*

GUARD A:

Here's Mi Chin-t'u.

Mi *kneels before the* Magistrate.

MAGISTRATE:

When I went to examine the corpse, I found it was a woman's. But the head is missing. Where did you hide the head?

CHIN-T'U:

I am falsely accused. Please, Your Honor, you cannot make me admit a crime that I have not committed.

MAGISTRATE:

Pretends to write on a parchment and hands it to the guards.

Guards, take this warrant and ask his teachers whether any of them is willing to guarantee for his conduct and have him released on probation.

GUARD A:

Yes, Your Honor.

He takes a slip of paper and goes out to upstage right.

MAGISTRATE:

Get up, Mi Chin-t'u. We'll wait for your teachers' word before we go any further with the trial.

Mi Chin-t'u *gets up and stands on the left side.*

Enter Guard A *from upstage and kneel before the* Magistrate.

GUARD A:

None of his teachers dares to guarantee for his conduct.

MAGISTRATE:

Guards, take off his headdress and gown.

Guards do so and Chin-*t'u, in a black gown with long white undersleeves and pony-tail like hair-do, kneels before the* Magistrate.

Now, Mi Chin-t'u. Since none of your teachers wants to vouch for your conduct, you must be a pretty bad character. Admit your murder. Confess. You'd better tell the truth, nothing but the truth.

CHIN-T'U:

Since I have not committed any crime, what can I confess?

MAGISTRATE:

I know you will not confess without torture. All right, guards. Beat him up. Give him fifty strokes.

The guards push Chin-t'u *on the floor and gesture to beat him.*

CHIN-T'U:

Wailing and moaning and trembling.

MAGISTRATE:

Are you going to admit your crime or not?

CHIN-T'U:

No.

MAGISTRATE:

Beat him up again. This time a hundred strokes.

CHIN-T'U:

All right, I will admit it.

MAGISTRATE:

Hurry up and confess.

CHIN-T'U:

Whatever you said is true.

MAGIATRATE:

Guards, put him in chains and take him to prison.

Enter Ma Yi *quietly from upstage right, goes to downstage right. He watches* Chin-t'u *being led away by the guards.*

MA YI:

Crying.

Grievance! Injustice! False accusation!

MAGISTRATE:

Who is that yelling of injustice and false accusation?

GUARDS:

An old man, Your Honor.

MAGISTRATE:

Bring him in.

GUARDS:

Going out of the court, to Ma Yi.

Come into the court, old man.

Ma Yi *enters the court and kneels before the* Magistrate *and stands on the left side.*

MAGISTRATE:

Why did you yell like that in front of the court? Don't you have any respect for the authorities?

MA YI:

How dare I show disrespect to the authorities? But a gross grievance has been done to my second master.

MAGISTRATE:

Who is your second master? And what grievance?

MA YI:

Allow me to tell you, Your Honor . My second master is Mi Chin-t'u. When I accompanied him to the capital to take the State Examination, one night at an inn we both had the same horrible dream. So we rushed home only to find that my first master was dead. After lamenting over the death of his brother the whole night, Second Master was arrested by two guards early the next morning, My second master did not do anything wrong. Please have mercy on him, Your Honor.

MAGISTRATE:

But your master has already admitted his crime.

MA YI:

O, so he has already admitted his crime. Your Honor, then you must be the more merciful to him.

MAGISTRATE:

You old fool! A crime is a crime and must be punished. How can I be merciful to a criminal?

Ma Yi *lowers his head in disappointment.*

But–I can see you are a very faithful servant. Therefore I will give you a chance to save your master's life. Since the head of the corpse is missing, if you can find the head within three days, you may be able to save his life.

Kneels in gratitude.

MA YI:

Thank you, Your Honor, thank you.

MAGISTRATE:

The court is dismissed.

Ma Yi *kowtows before the Magistrate.* The Magistrate *gets up and walks to Downstage Center and exits to upstage left with two Attendants.*

MA YI:

Kneeling.

Your Honor, have mercy, please, Your Honor, have mercy on my master!

GUARDS:

His Honor is gone and the court is dismissed.

The guards go out to upstage right.

MA YI:

Getting up.

Thank you, Your Honor.

Singing "erh huang Yao pan" from tape.

What a fine magistrate! He has given me a chance to save my master's life by finding the missing head within three days. But who was the murderer that was so cruel as to chop off the head? Where can I find the head ? Where can I find it? What am I going to do?

Thinking.

I've got it. I'll go home and talk it over with my wife and see if I can talk her into getting our only daughter's head to save my master's life.

Crossing the threshold.

That's exactly what I am going to do.

He goes out to upstage right.

SCENE EIGHT

The home of Ma Yi. *The next day.*

The setting is about the same as Scene One.

Enter Mama Ma *from upstage right and walks to downstage center. She is a stout woman, about fifty, dressed in a gray jacket and black skirt. Her face is round and expresses kindness and good nature, but years of toil.*

MAMA MA:

My husband has been away from home for many days and I'm worried about him.

Goes to sit on the chair which is placed in front of the table by the property man.

Enter Ma Yueh-hsiang *from upstage right and walks to downstage right. She is a charming girl of 17, wearing a black jacket and a long, beautifully pleated white skirt. Her hair is decorated with many flowers.*

MA YUEH-HSIANG:

I had a horrible dream last night. I must tell my mother about it.

Bows to Mama Ma *and sits at the left.*

Enter Ma Yi *with a dagger in hand, from upstage right and goes to downstage right.*

MA YI:

Aside.

Alas, alas: My child! When I think of it, I can't help crying. It's like a thousand swords thrusting into me. In despair, I'm returning to my hut. Oh, how can I face my family this way!

Mama *and* Yueh-hsiang *step over the imaginary doorsill to come out of the house and see* Ma Yi.

MAMA:

Ah, Papa!

Ma Yi *hides the dagger in his sleeve and steps over the doorsill into the house, followed by his wife and daughter.*

MA YI:

Aside.

I must not let Mama know this yet.

They all sit, Ma Yi *on the left,* Mama *on the right.*

YUEH HSIANG:

Bows.

Greetings to my father.

MA YI:

All right, my child, sit down.

Yueh-hsiang sits on the right, next to Mama.

MAMA:

Papa, when did you come back from your trip?

Pause.

Papa, what time did you come back?

Ma Yi *is so absorbed in meditation that he does not hear her. She speaks louder.*

Papa, when did you come back?

MA YI:

Hm . . . what . . . what did you say?

MAMA:

I asked you several times. When did you come back?

MA YI:

I came back yesterday.

MAMA:

Well, you are certainly acting in a peculiar way. What's the matter?

MA YI:

Getting up and brings Mama Ma *to downstage left.*

Mama, haven't you heard of my second master's trouble?

MAMA:

No, what happened to him?

MA YI:

Shhh! This is confidential. While I was staying at the inn with my second master on our way to the capital for him to take the advanced examinations, we both had the same horrible dream. So we rushed back to the master's house only to find that the elder master was dead! My second master kept watch over the coffin through the night, and at dawn some court guards came to arrest him on a charge of murder. He is falsely accused of seducing his widowed sister-in-law and killing her when she struggled. In the court he was tortured until he admitted his alleged crime.

MAMA:

Ai-ya, poor second master! He has always been kind to us. You must think of a way to save him.

MA YI:

That's just it. I asked the magistrate about it, and he told me the only way I could save my master was by finding the head of the corpse. Only the head will prove its identity.

MAMA:

You've got to find the head!

MA YI:

Ai-ya! Mama, how can I find this head without any clue, without any trace? There's only one way I can think of . . perhaps . the only way . . . and that is to kill our daughter and show them her head.

Ma Yi *throws the dagger on the floor stage center.*

Yueh-hsiang *jumps up and looks at the dagger in fright.*

MAMA:

Horrified, goes over to Yueh-hsiang.

Now, Papa, you know that we aren't young people anymore. We are both over fifty and have no son. Our daughter is all we have. Kill her? A thousand times no!

YUEH-HSIANG:

Approaches Ma Yi *and kowtows.*

Father, I don't mind being killed for such a noble cause, but when you both die, who will mourn for you?

Weeps.

Who will take care of the funeral?

MAMA:

Papa, I don't mind my daughter being killed, but who will sweep our graves and burn incense for our souls?

Yueh-hsiang weeps louder.

MAMA:

Helping Yueh-hsiang get up.

My child, don't cry. Let me persuade your father not to do it.

MA YI:

Mama, that second master has been very kind to me. We have to remember that a drop of kindness should be returned a fountainfold.

Mama *and* Yueh-hsiang *weep.*

The weeping of mother and daughter is sad indeed. It would soften a heart of stone. How can I ever raise this dagger to kill my own daughter!

Picks up dagger and comes close to Yueh-hsiang.

O, Heaven, harden my heart while I cut off the head of my beloved child!

Mama excitedly comes between him and Yueh-hsiang.

Ah, my dear daughter, whether you live or die will depend upon how you yourself use this heartless dagger. I cannot do it!

Throws the dagger on the floor and goes to the left. Mama *runs after him to appeal for mercy.*

YUEH-HSIANG:

Alone, on the left.

When I see the dagger on the dusty floor, I gather up courage. Yes, let me kill myself and save my father from this gruesome task. Let me cry one bitter cry . . . Father, Mother . . . farewell, farewell! It's a matter of only a second . . in a second . . . I'll be in another world.

Dances as she sings; then thrusts the dagger into her heart and falls. Mama, *a moment later, sees her and is alarmed.*

MAMA:

Ai-ya! Papa, my child has stabbed herself!

Runs toward Yueh-hsiang *and falls on the body, crying in anguish. She stands in front of* Yueh-hsiang, *with her back to the audience and her left hand raised as* Yueh-hsiang *gets up and goes out to upstage right.*

MA YI:

Going to the right.

Ah, alas, alas! My poor child! My only daughter is dead! How it breaks my heart! Oh, woe is me! But what can I do now? It's your head that will save my master's life! Yes, your head, my poor daughter.

Picks up the dagger and bends over the body, as the Property Man throws a red bundle on the floor and he picks it up as the head. He gestures to cross the threshold and exits to upstage left while Mama walks slowly and sadly out to upstage right.

SCENE NINE

The scene is the same as Scene Seven. Enter from upstage right the four Attendants. followed by the Magistrate *who walks to Downstage Center.*

MAGISTRATE:

Because of this headless murder case, I have been restless and preplexed for days.

Walks upstage and takes his seat.

Come, guards, bring in Mi Chin-t'u.

Guard A *exits to bring in* Chin-t'u *who enters from upstage left and kneels before the* Magistrate.

CHIN-T'U:

Kneeling.

Your Honor, Salutations!

MAGISTRATE:

For the hundredth time, where did you hide your sister-in-law's head? You' d better tell me quickly or I'll have you beaten again.

CHIN-T'U:

This is really and truly a false accusation. I did not kill my sister-in-law and I did not cut off her head How in the world do you expect me to know where her head is? Please have mercy, Your Honor, I did not commit the murder.

MAGISTRATE:

I must use torture to make you confess. Guards, employ the torture in the first degree. Or answer me now. Where is the missing head?

Enter Ma Yi *from the upstage right with a head represented by a red bundle.*

MA YI:

Coming to downstage right.

Here is the head!

GUARD A:

The head is here. Someone has found the head.

MAGISTRATE:

Bring him in and present the head before me.

Guard A leads in Ma Yi who kneels before the Magistrate. Guard A hands the head to the Magistrate who looks at it closely.

Guards, take Mi Chin-t'u back to prison.

CHIN-T'U:

Standing up and facing Ma Yi.

Instead of saving my life, you have made the situation worse for me.

Exit Chin-t'u with the guards to upstage left.

MA YI:

Kneeling.

Ai-ya, I don't understand.

Kneels.

Your Honor,

Gets up and stands on the left.

You told me the only possible way to save my master was to find the missing head. I have found the head for you now. Why did you put my second master back to prison?

MAGISTRATE:

Because this head doesn't belong to the body, you stupid old fool!

MA YI:

How can you tell?

MAGISTRATE:

This head's too young for the body. A pretty girl's head doesn't go with a middle-aged woman's body. With the head missing, this case was more or less a puzzle. But now, with this head, you have made the case more complicated. What's more, you have proved your master's guilt. Where did you get this head? Now speak up.

MA YI:

Kneels.

Ai-ya, Your Honor. It was like this, when you told me I could save my master's life by finding the missing head, I was grateful to you. But where could I find the missing head without a clue? What could I, an old man like me, do? So I went home and talked it over with my wife. The result was that I killed my only daughter to save my master's life.

MAGISTRATE:

O you! How could you do such a cruel and stupid thing? If you could kill your own daughter and cut off her head, I can see it would not have been difficult for Mi Chin-t'u to kill his sister-in-law. But the court will pardon you for your faithfulness to your master. You'd better go and have a coffin ready for your master. So after the execution, you can put him in the coffin and bury him. That will certainly be doing him a service.

Stands up and exits with the four Attendants to the left.

MA YI:

Have mercy, Your Honor, please have mercy.

GUARD A:

His Honor is gone and the court is dismissed.

MA YI:

Turning to face the audience, still kneeling.

But what did His Honor say?

GUARD B:

His Honor said that by trying to save your master's life, you have only proved his guilt.

MA YI:

Why? How?

GUARD A:

The head you brought in is too young for the body. So in trying to save your master's life you have proved that he is guilty of murder, and he is sentenced to death.

MA YI:

Ai-ya!

Shaking his head and beard, raising and trembling both sleeves, he falls on the floor and faints.

GUARD B:

There goes another corpse.

The two Guards *go out to the upstage left.*

MA YI:

Awakening from the trance singing hsi p'i yao pan *from tape.*

Ai ya ya – my master is going to die. What shall I do?

Thinking.

I have sacrificed my own dear daughter to no purpose.

Thinking.

I have got it. I hear that Grand Tutor Wen *(Clasps hands to show respect)* is a very just and upright Prime Minister. It is said that he has an extra eye to see the truth. By the Imperial Order, he is going to make inspections over all the country. I hear he will be coming to this county soon. I must go to see him at once before he arrives. Yes, that may be the only way to save my master's life.

Gestures to go out of the courtroom downstage center and exits to upstage left.

SCENE TEN

Late afternoon, the same day.

The scene is laid in the court of the Grand Tutor. Enter from upstage right four military guards and the Grand Tutor goes to sit in chair on top of a table to denote his seat of judgment. The four military guards stand, two on each side. They are dressed in armor and are holding spears, standing at attention, The Grand Tutor has a gold painted face, with a hooped-like jade belt and highsoled boots.

GRAND TUTOR:

By order of the Emperor, I, Grand Tutor Wen, am to see that homage is paid by foreign states and that justice is upheld within the empire. No convicts shall escape and no injustice, grievances, or wrongs shall not be righted. Today is the 369th day. Guards, put out the placard so people will know they come now to plead for justice.

A guard with a gong in hand walks downstage center over the doorsill and then to downstage left. Enter Ma Yi *from upstage right.*

MA YI:

I have sacrificed my only beloved daughter with the intention of saving my master's life, but alas, I have only made the situation worse. Finding a head for the corpse only proves his guilt. Ah, I am defeated!

Pause.

Now I am ready to sacrifice my own life for him. Let me go to Grand Tutor Wen and plead for justice.

Going to the left and beating the gong.

A grievance!

Big gong.

Injustice!

Big gong.

Let's have justice!

Big gong.

GRAND TUTOR:

Guard, bring him before me.

Two guards bring Ma Yi *before the Grand Tutor.* Ma Yi *kowtows before the* Grand Tutor *and presents him with a scroll of written accusations.*

MA YI:

I appeal to you, honorable Grand Tutor, to right the wrong done by the Magistrate of Mo Li County.

Grand Tutor *reads the written accusations,* Ma Yi *stands on left.*

GRAND TUTOR:

Putting the scroll aside–

What impertinence! You dare to file a complaint against the magistrate of Mo Li County! Are you familiar with the imperial laws?

MA YI:

Kneels.

It is because of the imperial laws that I dare to call for justice.

GRAND TUTOR:

I have the torture of the hammer and the copper lever knife ready. Do you still dare to make the charge?

MA YI:

Do I dare? Torture or not, I must file my complaint.

GRAND TUTOR:

Guards, bring the lever knife.

Guards *carrying in the lever knife and put* Ma Yi *in the opening of the machine, the front of which has the shape of a tiger's head with a wide-opened mouth.*

MA YI:

Being on the floor, with one foot up and the right sleeve raised and trembling.

To save my master's life, I am willing to suffer any kind of torture. Oh, Grand Tutor, exert your power to right this terrible wrong.

GRAND TUTOR:

To himself with his right sleeve raised at face level.

Ma Yi is not a bit afraid of the hammer and lever knife. There must truly be a legitimate grievance here.

To the guards.

Release him.

To Ma Yi.

Now, Ma Yi, this kind of torture doesn't frighten you, eh? We still have some thirty-six heavenly nails. Do you still dare to file the accusation?

MA YI:

Thirty-six heavenly nails? Ha! If you put me into a caldron of boiling oil or on a mountain of sharp swords, I would still file this charge!

GRAND TUTOR:

Guards, take him away!

The guards drag Ma Yi *out by upstage left*

Carry in the heavenly nails and prepare incense for the gods.

The guards bring in a board bristling with nails and set a pot of incense before it.

Music from tape or big gong and cymbals.

Grand Tutor Wen *comes down from the table and bows with his hands clasped before the board of nails, and then goes back to his seat.* Guards *drag in* Ma Yi *from upstage left, now naked to the waist.*

MA YI:

Heaven! Oh, heaven! What have I done to deserve this? All I'm trying to do is right a wrong for my master, and I must suffer all this! Oh, Heaven, help me!

Music sounds and Ma Yi *is tossed up and down on the board of nails by the guards.*

GRAND TUTOR:

Enough! Now carry him out.

Two guards carry Ma Yi *with blood on his chest out to upstage left.*

Here's the document of the case.

Grand Tutor Wen *hands a scroll to a guard who exits to upstage right.*

Let me sleep awhile. Guards, do not go far away.

Guards exit to the right and left and the Grand Tutor *rests his head on his arm and falls asleep. Lights dim. Three strokes are sounded, meaning one o'clock in the morning. Enter the ghosts of* Mi Chin-t'u's *brother,* Ma Yi's *daughter, and* Mistress Li *from upstage right accompanied by slow beats of the big gong.*

The women wear red veils to show they are headless.

They walk in, one by one, in a dreamlike, flowing manner.

MI CHIN-CHING:

Downstage right.

I am Mi Chin-ching's ghost. I was murdered by my wife and her paramour. Let me beg Grand Tutor Wen to right the wrong for me.

Goes to knowtow before the Grand Tutor *and exits to upstage left.*

MISTRESS LI:

Downstage right.

I am Mistress Li's ghost. I was murdered by my husband and his paramour. Let me beg Grand Tutor Wen to right the grievance for me.

Goes to kneel before the Grand Tutor *and exits to upstage left.*

YUEH-HSIANG:

Downstage right.

I am the ghost of Ma Yueh-hsiang. I killed myself to help my father save his master's life, but in vain. Let me beg Grand Tutor Wen to do justice.

Goes to kneel before the Grand Tutor *and exits to upstage left.*

Suddenly an actor dressed like a monkey, with a flower in its mouth, leaps on stage from upstage right (music) and jumps around. The Grand Tutor *looks at it in surprise. Exit the monkey to upstage left.*
right.

GRAND TUTOR:

Getting up.

Ah, it's already one o'clock in the morning. What a strange dream I had! Three ghosts pleading with me to right a wrong. Later a monkey with a flower in its mouth came jumping before me.

Sits down again.

There must be a man involved in this crime . . . a man who looks like a monkey . . . maybe his name is Flowery-Mouth Monkey . . . or . . . Monkey Flower Mouth . . . a puzzle.

Pause.

There is only one way to solve the mystery. I will personally go to Mo Li County and investigate this matter.

Jumping up.

Guards, guards!

Enter four guards from left and right.

A GUARD:

Yes, Your Excellency!

GRAND TUTOR:

Light up the lanterns and let us start for Mo Li County at once!

The guards get the lanterns from the Property Man
All go off to upstage left.

SCENE ELEVEN

A moment later.
The scene is before the courtroom in Mo Li *County. Four strokes are heard, denoting three o'clock in the morning.*
Enter four guards leading Mi Chin-t'u *in chains from the right*

GUARD:

It is now three o'clock in the morning.

At the stroke of five, at dawn, by the order of the magistrate, Mi Chin-t'u is to be executed without fail.

All go off to upstage left.
Five strokes are sounded, but no dawn is in sight.
Enter from upstage right two watchmen, one holding a wooden gong to sound the hours and another holding a lamp.

WATCHMAN A:

So! We have already struck five strokes[1] and yet no dawn is in sight. I wonder why!

WATCHMAN B:

If dawn doesn't come, we still must sound the hour.

They both beat six strokes.
Both go off to upstage left.
A moment later, seven . . . then eight . . . strokes are heard.
Re-enter the two watchmen from upstage right.

---

1. One stroke nine o'clock at night
Two strokes eleven o'clock
Three strokes one o'clock in the morning
Four strokes three o'clock
Five strokes five o'clock

WATCHMAN A:

The eighth stroke was struck and it is now time to mark the ninth. In my forty years of marking the hours at night, this is the strangest thing I have ever seen!

WATCHMAN B:

There must be a reason! Heaven has a reason for everything. Let us sound the ninth stroke eventhough dawn refuses to come.

The two watchmen exit to upstage left, as they begin to strike the nine strokes.

SCENE TWELVE

At the sound of the ninth stroke, from upstage right enter four guards followed by the Grand Tutor *who goes to seat himself in the center of the stage in front of a table.* The Magistrate *enters and kowtows before the* Grand Tutor.

GRAND TUTOR:

Are you the magistrate of Mo Li County?

MAGISTRATE:

Bowing his head.

Yes, Your Excellency.

GRAND TUTOR:

Why don't you raise your head?

MAGISTRATE:

Because I have done wrong, Your Excellency.

GRAND TUTOR::

Consider yourself pardoned.

MAGISTRATE:

Thank you, Your Excellency.

Raises his head, gets up to stand on left.

GRAND TUTOR:

Ah, so you have tortured one Mi Chin-t'u to admit his alleged crime, and his servant, Ma Yi, has filed a complaint against you for false accusation.

MAGISTRATE:

It was lack of judgment on my part. I plead for your pardon.

GRAND TUTOR:

To the guards.

Bring Mi Chin-t'u in.

A guard goes out by upstage left and then returns with Mi Chin-t'u, *who kneels by the side of the* Magistrate *before the* Grand Tytor.

CHIN-T'U:

My salutations to Your Excellency.

Kowtows.

GRAND TUTOR:

Tell me truthfully about your case.

CHIN-T'U:

I had a terrible dream on my way to take a government examination in the capital. So my servant, Ma Yi, and I rushed home only to find my elder brother had already died. Then the next morning, I was accused of seducing and murdering my widowed sister-in-law! O, I am innocent, Your Excellency! Have mercy on me!

GRAND TUTOR:

Mi Chin-t'u, go into the next room for the present.

Exit Mi Chin-t'u *to upstage left*

Magistrate, who reported this murder to you?

MAGISTRATE:

A man by the name of Monkey Flower Mouth.

GRAND TUTOR:

Ah, it must be he.

Surprised at the mention of that name. Slowly and half to himself raising his right sleeve to face level.

Aloud.

Seize Monkey Flower Mouth and bring him here!

The Magistrate gets up by the wave of Grand Tutor Wen's *sleeve.*

The guards exit to upstage right and bring in Monkey.

MONKEY:

What's wrong? Why have you brought me here? Oh, there are so many people! Something must have gone wrong. How can I ever escape!

Kneels before the Grand Tutor.

My salutations to you, Your Excellency.

GRAND TUTOR:

Monkey Flower Mouth, how did you commit the murder? Deny nothing. Confess it all!

MONKEY:

I don't know anything about the murder! What murder?

GRAND TUTOR:

You will not confess without torture, eh? Guards, make preparations for his torture.

Four guards approach Monkey, menacingly.

MONKEY:

Trembling.

Wait! Wait! I will confess! Your Excellency, I, Monkey Flower Mouth, am the lover of Mi Chin-t'u's sister-in-law, Mistress Yao. We plotted and killed Mi's brother, Mi Chin-ch'ing, but soon Chin-t'u returned. Yao was afraid he might discover the murder, so we schemed again. We killed my wife, cut off her head, and dressed her in Yao's clothes. We put the body at Mi's back door. I reported to the Magistrate that Mi had seduced and killed Yao.

GRAND TUTOR:

What brutality! What a horrible monster you are! Bring Mistress Yao before me.

Two guards leave by upstage right and bring in Yao.

YAO:

To Monkey.

What are you doing here?

MONKEY:

They brought me here. I have already confessed everything, so you'd better . do the same!

YAO:

Kneels before the Grand Tutor.

My salutations, Your Excellency.

GRAND TUTOR:

How did you murder your husband? Speak up!

YAO:

Slyly glancing at the judge–

It was all the evil doing of Monkey Fower Mouth. I had nothing to do with it.

GRAND TUTOR:

A little torture will make you speak the truth! Guards, prepare!

YAO:

With trembling and raised handkerchief.

Oh, wait a moment, a moment! I will confess!

MONKEY:

Confess quickly!

YAO:

I confess to committing the same crimes as Monkey Flower Mouth.

GRAND TUTOR:

Guards, let them sign the confession.

Monkey and Yao sign a scroll.

Give them due punishment. Monkey Flower Mouth shall be executed slowly by the lever knife and Mistress Yao by having her stomach slit open. Take them away!

MONKEY:

If we must die, let us die together!

Guards take them both out to upstage left.

GRAND TUTOR:

Magistrate of Mo Li County, go back to your office and wait for further word from me.

MAGISTRATE:

Downstage left, filliping the sweat from his brow.

Thank heaven, this case is closed.

Exits to upstage left.

GRAND TUTOR:

Bring in Mi Chin-t'u and Ma Yi.

The guards exit to upstage left and upstage right and return with Mi Chin-t'u *back in his fine clothes and hat from upstage left and* Ma Yi *also back in his gown and hat from upstage right.*

MA YI:

Ai-ya, my dear master!

Weeps

They both come before Grand Tutor Wen, kneel and stand on either side.

GRAND TUTOR:

Ma Yi, you are indeed a faithful servant. I respect you for your great loyalty. May I ask if you have any son of your own?

MA YI:

I have no son, but one daughter who is now dead.

GRAND TUTOR:

Mi Chin-t'u, you have been set free mainly through the heroic efforts of your faithful servant. I suggest you take him as your adopted father, and care for him in his old age. You will be able to sweep his grave after his death. What do you think of my suggestion?

CHIN-T'U:

I am honored, Your Excellency.

GRAND TUTOR:

Then slaute and greet him as your adopted father.

CHIN-T'U:

My father, I kowtow to you.

Kneels and kowtows.

MA YI:

Embarrassed and pleased, trying to help Mi *get up.*

Oh, how can I stand such ceremony!

GRAND TUTOR:

Mi Chin-t'u, now go home and study hard. A bright future is in store for you. I will help you whenever I can. Now, take your father home.

MA YI and CHIN-T'U:

Thank you, Your Excellency!

They go off stage to upstage right.

GRAND TUTOR:

Guards, lead the way to the execution grounds. After these two murderers are punished and done away with, we shall go to another place to see if any other injustices exist.

Music.

All circle around the stage and go off to upstage left.

CURTAIN

THE PRICE OF WINE

(Mei Lung Chen)

This is a comedy, a wholehearted, light comedy. A great favorite with the Chinese audience, *The Price of Wine* affords an opportunity for the *tan* and scholarly *sheng* actors to display their skills. The sprightly wit and folksy humor in this Capital Opera have popularized it with the masses.

The Chinese title is *Mei Lung Chen* (梅龍鎭), or "Plum Dragon Town." "Dragon" symbolizes the emperor and "plum" is synonomous with pleasure, so the title actually means "the town in which the emperor enjoys himself." There is yet another Chinese name for this Capital Opera, an adaptation by Dr. Ch'i Ju-shan, entitled *Yu Lung Hsi Feng* (游龍戲鳳). It means "The Traveling Dragon Teases a Phoenix." The "Feng" phoenix is the female of the species and is a term used by Chinese to indicate a gorgeous lady. From this discussion of the titles, it is easy to divine the simple plot of this play, although a foreigner will be surprised at some of the developments in the plot and learn much of Chinese mores in the process of reading.

The Price of Wine is believed to have been written in the Ming dynasty, probably to flatter the emperor at the time, Cheng Teh (1506-1522).

This play was produced with great success by the American students in my Chinese drama class at Grinnell College, Grinnell, Iowa, in November, 1963 and in December, of the same year at the State University of Iowa, Iowa City. The costumes used were all made of local materials and by the students under my supervision. The students of the Art Department and of the Music Department lent a helping hand in this production. Three students from the Music Departement were present at every rehearsal for more than two months for almost all the movements were timed by percussions. It was a most enjoyable and rewarding experience for both the audience and the performer. They realized that the Chinese classical drama is not realistic but fluid. From the laughter, warm and hearty applause, one could easily see that the simplicity of this theatrical art–the stylized movements, spoken lines and song–had actually carried across to the American audience the humor and vitality of this Peking opera play, *The Price of Wine.*

In March, 1970 this play was produced with greater success by the Taipei International Women's Club. It is with the hope that more productions will be made in every corner of the world for the understanding of the aspirations, thoughts and feelings of the Chinese people.

THE PRICE OF WINE
Characters

EMPEROR CHENG TEH. . a famous emperor of the Ming dynasty; aged 35.
(正 德 皇 帝)

LI FENG . . . . the beautiful sister of an innkeeper; aged 17.
(李 鳳)

Scene I:

The anteroom on a small inn in the town of the Plum Dragon. An evening in spring.

Scene II:

The setting is the same. The center stage, however, is now Li Feng's bedroom. Later in the same evening.

The Setting

The anteroom of a small inn in the town of the Plum Dragon. The stage is almost bare, with back and side curtains for background. In the center of the stage stands a table, on which are placed an unlit red candle to indicate that it is night, a small wine cup and a wooden block. A chair is in front of it and another one is on upstage right. The table and chairs have red coverings with painted yellow floral designs.

Downstage on the left sit the musicians facing the right side of stage: the Little Drummer, the Little-gong and-wooden-clapper player and the big-gong-and cymbal player, who time almost every movement of the actors throughout the performance. *Ta Kuo Men* or overture for a Chinese opera is played from a record or tape.

The music may be omitted if an appropriate record or tape is not available.

SCENE ONE

At Rise:

Cheng Teh, *tall and handsome, enters from upstage right. He is disguised as a soldier in the military uniform of the Ming dynasty: a long blue kimono gown, fastened under the right arm, with a white collar and long white undersleeves. He wears a long black artificial beard, a black soft hat with yellow painted designs, two yellow tassels on either side and a big red flower in front, and a red hood with yellow lining over the back of the headdress. He wears a pair of black boots with white high soles. He carries a folded fan which he uses often to fan himself in meditation or in satisfaction. After coughing "Ah pei" to show his dignity, he takes square steps in the accompaniment of the big gong, little drum and cymbals and little gong, little drum and cymbals. When he comes half way on the stage, he tidies his headdress and beard and waves his two long sleeves. He then walks to downstage center.*

CHENG TEH:

I have left my palace to seek wise men among the commoners and to find out the actual conditions of my state.

drum and gong.

Also, it will give me a chance to see for myself the famous beauty spots in my kingdom.

Goes to the chair in front of the table and sits.

I (little gone) Emperor Cheng Teh of the Ming dynasty, *(pause)* am alone here in this little Li Lung Inn, in the town of the Plum Dragon. Whenever I knock on the table with this wooden horse, I will be served tea or wine.

4 little drum beats.

Since I have entrusted the nobles of my court with state affairs, I have some time to enjoy myself. Put *(3 little drum beats)* I'm lonesome *(2 drum beats)* very lonesome!

Shaking his head

Gets up and sings as the property man puts the chair behind the

table. He goes and sits down.
He knocks on the table with the wooden horse.
Drum and 2 wooden clapper beats.

Hey, innkeeper!

LI FENG:

Off stage.

Coming!

Li Feng, *carrying a tray on her left hand and a big pink handkerchief in the other, enters from the audience's left. She is a pretty young girl, charming and lively. She wears a green jacket, green trousers, and a pink apron with a long sash. She has flowers and brilliants on her hair. She walks with graceful and mincing steps with the accompaniment of the little drum and little gong. Halfway on the stage, she waves her big silk handkerchief from one side to another. She sings" erh huang-ping-pan," (from the tape or record from the original Chinese opera play) as if she were really singing as she dances around the right side of the front stage which is the backyard. She dances to the front stage center.*

I was born and brought up in Plum Dragon town. My brother told me there's a soldier in the anteroom. Now, I'll serve him some tea.

She turns around and lifts her left foot to cross the imaginary threshold, accompanied by the little drum and little gong. She walks to the right side of Cheng Teh *and puts down the tray on the table.*

Cheng Teh *sees her, gets up, and laughs.*

Ha,Ha! Ha! Ha!

LI FENG:

Blushing and walking quickly away to the front stage.

Ai-ya-ya!
I'd better hurry back to my room and finish my sewing.

Cheng Teh *walks up and deliberately steps on* Li Feng's *long sash. He holds it firmly while she struggles to free herself. She tries to pull away three times, then finally,* Li Feng *cries "Look!" and points behind* Cheng Teh, *who thinks someone is coming and*

Cheng Teh steps on Li Feng's long sash to prevent her from leaving.

lets loose of the sash. Li Feng *slips out again lifting her right foot to cross the threshold and runs offstage at the right.*

CHENG TEA:

Laughing.

Ha, ha! Ha, ha! Ha, ha, ha, ha! What a pity such a beautiful, dainty flower should be allowed to grow up in a remote, unsophisticated market town. Amazing that my good nobles haven't discovered her for me!

He goes back to his chair.

Sings "erh-huang-ping-pan" from tape.

Let me sound the wooden horse for the second time.

Knocks again with the accompaniment of the drum and the gong.

Li Feng *enters from upstage right, and walks downstage center.*

Crossing the threshold to enter the room.

LI FENG:

Here comes the innkeeper!

She walks toward Cheng Teh's left.

CHENG TEH:

Big Brother[1] Innkeeper! Big Brother Innkeeper!

LI FENG:

Going away to the front stage.

There is no Big Brother Innkeeper–only a Big Sister Innkeeper.

CHENG TEH:

Aside.

Ah, ai-ya! This little lassie calls herself Big Sister Innkeeper. I'll call her that and see how she reacts!

He nods and fans himself.

Aloud.

Big Sister! Big Sister!

---

1. The Chinese custom to show respect or intimacy is to use the terms Big Brother and Big Sister.

LI FENG:

Comes back to him and stands with her left hand on her hip on the left side of table.

Yes, Mister Soldier, what can I do for you?

CHENG TEH:

I want to know; who is that tall, slim young man who was here just now?

LI FENG:

He's my brother.

CHENG TEH:

What's his name?

LI FENG;

Li Lung.

CHENG TEH:

Big Sister, what's your name?

LI FENG:

I? I don't have a name.

Takes a few steps forward and bends her head.

CHENG TEH:

Strokes his beard and fans himself.

Why, everyone has a name. How is it possible you don't have one?

LI FENG:

Well, I have one, but I don't want to tell you.

Points coquettishly at him.

If I do, you will call me by name, and I don't like it.

Waves her big handkerchief and has both her hands on her hips.

CHENG TEH:

I promise you I will not call you by your name.

LI FENG:

Walks up to him.

You know my surname is Li, don't you?

LI FENG:

Stands with her left hand on her hip.

Feng, which means phoenix.

CHENG TEH:

What an exquisite name!

Shakes beard and closes his eyes dreamily and meditatively.

Oh, Li Feng,

Three beats on the little drun.

Li Feng!

Three beats on the little drum.

LI FENG:

Angrily stamps her foot.

Now give it back to me!

Walks around to his left.

CHENG TEH:

Give back? What is it you want me to return?

LI FENG:

My name!

Little gong.

Give me back my name!

Stamps her foot.

CHENG TEH:

The name is still yours, but once a word is uttered, it blows away like the wind. How can I return it to you?

LI FENG:

But just now you promised me you wouldn't call me by my name.

Little gong.

Why did you do it?

Little drum and little gong.

CHENG TEH:

Oh, I see. All right, I won't call you by your name any more, Big Sister.

LI FENG:

Walks to his right.

You mustn't do it again.
Now what can I do for you?

CHENG TEH:

Ah, Big Sister, what kind of wine and food do you serve here?

LI FENG:

In a businesslike manner, she puts up three fingers in her left hand.

We serve three classes of wine and food here.

CHENG TEH:

What are they?

LI FENG:

In the same tone.

High class, *[puts up her thumb in the right hand (big gong)]* middle class, *[puts up her third finger in the left hand (little gong)]* and low class, *[puts up her little finger in the right hand. (two beats of the little drum and one faint beat of the little gong)]*

CHENG TEH:

Serve me first class food and wine.

LI FENG:

First class food and wine are for the officials.

CHENG TEH:

Then what about middle class?

LI FENG:

That's for the merchants.

CHENG TEH:

Who is the low class for?

LI FENG:

Low class?

Walks away and coyly holds up her handkerchief with her left hand.

I don't want to tell you.

CHENG TEH:

Why don't you tell me?

LI FENG:

Because *3 beats on the little drum* because I'm afraid you'll be offended.

Big gong.

CHENG TEH:

I promise I won't be offended.

LI FENG:

Goes to his left side.

Are you sure you won't be angry with me?

CHENG TEH:

Firmly.

I won't.

LI FENG:

Takes a few steps away from him.

All right, I'll tell you. The low class is for people like you– *(points to him)*– soldiers who live on our taxes!

She puts her hands on her hips.

CHENG TEH:

Stands up and holds up his left sleeve.

Aside.

Ah, ai-ya! So soldiers are to be ill-treated. All right, when I return to the court, I'll give a million pieces of gold to the armed forces as a special bonus.

Goes to Li Feng:

Big Sister, please serve me high-class wine and food.

LI FENG:

Looking at Cheng Teh *with suspicious scorn, up and down accompanied by the little drum.*

So you want high-class food and wine, eh?

Big gong.

CHENG TEH:

Exactly.

LI PENG:

Let me ask you a riddle and see if you can figure it out.

CHENG TEH:

Go ahead!

He goes back to his seat.

LI FENG:

She comes and stands on his right.

Before you go on board the ship,

Little gong.

CHENG TEH:

You must pay for the passage.

Big gong.

LI FENG:

When you spend a night at an inn,

Little gong.

CHENG TEH:

You must pay for the lodging.

Big gong.

LI FENG·

Now if you want to have a drink.

little gong.

CHENG TEH:

You just drink your fill.

Big gong.

LI FENG:

Pshaw! You can't even say, "You must pay for the wine." "Drink your fill, ha!"

She waves her big handkerchief at him and she puts her hands on hip.

Big gong twice.

CHENG TEH:

Stands up.

Are you insinuating you want *me* to pay *you* for the wine?

LI FENG:

It's not *I* who wants *you* to pay.

CHENG TEH:

Then who wants me to pay?

LI FENG:

When my brother comes back, he will ask me for the money.

CHENG TEH:

If you want money, *it's* easy.

Sits down.

Roll up the screen and let the moonlight shine through the door.

LI FENG:

Yes, Mister Soldier.

She goes to the downstage center and gestures to roll up an imaginary screen, ties the strings and then comes back to the table. All movements are accompanied by the little drum and the little gong.

Cheng Teh *gets up and walks in front of table.*

CHENG TEH:

I take out a piece of silver
To pay Big Sister for the wine.
Now take it. *(Little gong and cymbals)*
He streches his hand to Li Feng.

LI FENG:

Put it on the table.

CHENG TEH:

The table is slippery
And the piece of silver is smooth.
If it falls on the floor,
It will be lost.

LI FENG:

If it falls on the floor,
I can easily pick it up.

CHENG TEH:

I'm afraid . . .
Little drum.

LI FENG:

What are your afraid of?

CHENG TEH:

I'm afraid you'll hurt your willowy waist.

LI FENG:

What is it to you if I should hurt my waist?

CHENG TEH:

I won't be able to bear it. It'll break my heart to see you harm yourself.

LI FENG:

If I can bear it, why can't you?

CHENG TEH:

Huh! You don't deserve my sympathy! Here, take it.

Little gong and cymbals.

Again he stretches out his hand but tries to cover her hand with his fan.

LI FENG:

I know–you don't want to part with the piece of silver!!

CHENG TEH:

I certainly am willing to part with it, but I'm afraid you don't want to take it from my hand.

LI FENG:

Goes downstage, near the footlights. Lifts her left hand to hide her face from Cheng Teh *to do the aside.*

Ai-ya! Let me see.

Circling her index finger in front of her right temple, accompanied by 3 beats on little drum and little gong.

It is obvious this soldier is not a gentlemen. Let me play a trick on him.

Goes back to Cheng Teh.

Have you seen the ancient paintings in our hotel?

CHENG TEH:

Ah, I love ancient paintings. Where are they?

Stands up.

LI FENG:

Pointing to the back of the stage–

3 little drum 1 gong.

There!

CHENG TEH:

Where?

3 beats on little drum and 1 gong.

As soon as Cheng Teh's *head is turned.* Li Feng *very quickly takes the piece of silver from his hand.*

LI FENG:

Triumphant and laughing.

Here!

(2 beats on little gong)

Showing the piece of silver on her palm–

CHENG TEH:

Turning around–

This little lass tricked me, after all!

He sits down again.

LI FENG:

Now that I have this piece of silver, may I ask how many plates I should serve?

CHENG TEH:

Waving his long sleeves.

One for me and one for my horse.

LI FENG:

This is too much silver to serve one person. It is too much, sir, too much.

CHENG TEH:

Meat and rice for me and hay for my horse.

Waving his left sleeve.

LI FENG:

It is still too much.

CHENG TEH:

Then go and buy some flowers for your hair with the rest.

LI FENG:

Thank you, sir. This way, please.

Takes the candle and points to the left at the back of stage.

CHENG TEH:

Stands up and follows Li Feng.

Where to?

LI FENG:

Crossing the "threshold" (3 beats on little drum and one beat on little gong)

This way to the dining room.

Pointing to left.

CHENG TEH:

Crossing the "threshold".

Let's go to your bedroom.

Pointing to right.

LI FENG:

Pointing to her left, seriously, firmly and slowly–

To the dining room!

(3 beats on little drum and 2 beats on Big gong)

CHENG TEH:

Ay? Dining room?

He points to his right.

Big sister, whose bedroom is that?

(1 Little gong, 2 beats on little drum and 1 little gong).

LI FENG:

It's mine.

CHENG TEH:

That's exactly where I want to go. Come on.

He starts to walk to the right.

LI FENG:

Very seriously and exactingly.

But Mr. Soldier, you know that men and women, in giving and taking things, should not touch even hands!

She hands the candle to Cheng Teh.

CHENG TEH:

Aside, lifting his left sleeve.

Hm! This country lass even knows the rudiments of etiquette. She knows that men and women should not touch hands when giving and taking things.

Laughing.

All right, I'll go to the *dining* room. The doors in this town of the Plum Dragon are stuck very tightly.

LI FENG:

Ay.

She pushes him toward the left and closes the door.

CHENG TEH:

Big sister, you are very tight, too!

Laughing, Cheng Teh *exits to the left.*

LI FENG:

Lets out a sigh and crosses the "threshold" to go into the room.

Ah-tsiu! I have closed the doors.

Erh Huang music.

She goes and sets the table with imaginary dishes, plates, and a pair of chopsticks and another candle provided by the property man, who appears and disappears immediately, accompanied by the soft playing of the cymbals or music.

I'd better set the table here. Now I'll call the soldier to dinner.

Going and calling to the left–

(accompanied by little drum)

What a funny fellow! When I asked him to go to that room just now, he didn't want to go. When I call him to come out, he is reluctant to leave it!

She turns to the right side of stage.

In preparing his dinner, I have dirtied my hands.

Let me go and wash them!

As Li Feng *gestures to wash hands, facing the right, accompanied by the little gong,* Cheng Teh *comes out from the left, crosses the threshold, tiptoes toward her as she pours the imaginary basin of water from, the window accompanied by the little drum, and embraces her. (Big gong and cymbals).* Li Feng *pushes him away.*

CHENG TEH:

Walking toward the left.

The people in this Plum Dragon Town are so proper!

LI FENG:

Approaching him.

Proper!

Little gong.

I'll hit you a plateful!

CHENG TEH:

Why all this abuse?

LI FENG:

Ever since you entered our inn, you have stared at me from head to toe. What is there about us women that you think is so good-looking?

CHENG TEH:

You are very good-looking, Big Sister, and I love to look at you.

LI FENG:

If you love to look, then look a few times.

With her right hand on her hip, she stands sedately and serenely before him.

CHENG TEH:

Big Sister is loosening up! That being the case, I'll look as closely and thoroughly as I can.

With his hands behind his back, he walks clockwise around Li Feng *and feasts his eyes on her, accompanied by the little drum and I beat on little drum and gong at the end.*

LI FENG:

Look at me again!

She puts both her hands on her hips.

CHENG TEH:

All right, I'll look again!

Walks counterclockwise around Li Feng.

Hmm good,

Little gong.

Splendid,

Cymbal,Cymbal.

Magnificent,

Big gong.

Incomparable model of excellence!

LI FENG:

She puts her left hand on her hip.

Look again!

CHENG TEH:

Enough, enough!

LI FENG:

If you weren't a customer in our inn, I'd curse you!

Puts both her hands on her hips angrily.

CHENG TEH:

Oh? You want to curse me?

LI FENG:

Not only curse you, but hit you!

Clapper and gong.

CHENG TEH:

I have never been hit by anyone since I was born. But if you, Big Sister, want to, hit me a few times.

LI FENG:

Raising her hand–

(4 beats on the little drum, crescendo)

Is that so? Then I want to hit you.

Li Feng *withdraws her hand blushingly. (4 beats on the little drum, diminuendo) Going to the right.*

Ai-ya-ya! I dare not do it.

CHENG TEH:

Why not?

LI FENG:

Because I'm afraid you'll be angry with me.

CHENG TEH:

I promise you I won't.

LI FENG:

If you won't be angry, then I'll . . .

Little drum.

Strikes Cheng Teh.

Hit . . . .

Little gong.

hit you . . .

2 little gong and cymbal.

Li Feng *runs, crosses the "threshold" and exits upstage right, accompanied by the little drum.*

CHENG TEH:

Bursts into laughter.

Ha! Ha! Ha! What a smart girl this Li Feng is! She can play tricks on me! Let me sound the wooden horse again.

He goes to sit down and knocks with the wooden horse (drum and gong) and Li Feng *enters, the little drum.*

LI FENG:

Walks downstage. To the audience.

The wine must be cold and the tea icy.

CHENG TEH:

Calling.

Miss Innkeeper! Miss Innkeeper!

LI FENG:

Crossing the "threshold." ,

Yes, Mister Soldier, Is your tea icy?

CHENG TEH:

My tea isn't icy.

LI FENG:

Then is your wine cold?

CHENG TEH:

My wine isn't cold.

LI FENG:

Huh! Your tea isn't icy and your wine isn't cold. Then why did you beat on our table? If you break it, you'll have to pay for it.

CHENG TEH:

You think I can't pay for the damage of a table? I can even pay for the damage of a person!

Big gong.

LI FENG:

Then which one do you want to pay for?

CHENG TEH:

Er . . .

Stroking his beard and fanning himself – 4 beats on Little Drum.

I want to pay for this table.

LI FENG:

In the first place, sir, let me ask you, why did you call me? What can I do for you?

CHENG TEH:

Big Sister, who set the table for dinner?

LI FENG:

I did. Wasn't it beautifully set?

Looking proudly at table.

CHENG TEH:

Yes, beautifully set, but it's a pity it lacks two things.

LI FENG:

What two things?

CHENG TEH:

Plum blossoms and white turnips!

Drum, one beat.

Powder and rouge, Erh . . .

Embarrassingly. (Drum, three beats.)

A beautiful lady of the moon!

LI FENG:

Oh, I see, sir, so you want some carrots and turnips. Wait, I'll get them for you.

Starts walking forward, one beat each step.

CHENG TEH:

Not those!

She stops and turns toward him.

LI FENG:

Then what do you mean?

CHENG TEH:

Ah, I mean those in pink aprons and green trousers like you.

LI FENG:

Oh, those! We used to have them around.

CHENG TEH:

How about now?

LI FENG:

Now the government prohibits them. It is said that there are none, but there are still some. However, where can I, a girl like me in the dark of night, find one for you?

CHENG TEH:

Moves his head in a circular movement and strokes his beard.

That's right, how and where could you find one in the dark of night? Since this is the case, Big Sister, I'd like to discuss something with you.

LI FENG:

What is it you want to discuss with me?

Goes to him.

CHENG TEH:

Will you do me the favor of pouring a cup of wine for me?

LI FENG:

I just sell wine–

Waving her handkerchief toward him

I don't pour it like a paid entertainer!

She puts both her hands on her hips.

CHENG TEH:

Oh, do pour!

LI FENG:

Turning and taking a step away from him.

No, I won't.

CHENG THE:

Are you going to pour or not?

LI FENG:

No!

1 clapper, putting her right hand on her hip.

No!

2 clapper, putting her left hand on her hip.

No!

3 clapper and gong, putting both her hands on her hips.

CHENG TEH:

All right, give me back the piece of silver!

LI FENG:

I'll get it.

Takes a few steps toward downstage center, little drum and little gong.

CHENG TEH:

Stands up.

Wait! I've eaten your dinner and drunk your wine. If your brother comes he'll ask you for the money. What are you going to tell him?

LI FENG:

Little drum and little gong. Worried, then aside.

Let me humor him a while.
Sir, what is the color of the rats in your village?

Goes back to him.

CHENG TEH:

Our rats are gray.

LI FENG:

Ours are white.

CHENG TEH:

Really? Where are they?

LI FENG:

There!

Pointing under the table.

CHENG TEH:

Looks under the table.

Where!

LI FENG:

Very swiftly pours wine into Cheng Teh's *cup.*
Here!

Points to the cup of wine.

CHENG TEH:

Who poured this wine for me?

LI FENG:

Triumphantly and coyly.
I!

CHENG TEH:

Huh! Such style of pouring wine! And only one cup! Even ten or twenty cups don't mean much, poured in such style!

LI FENG:

Then how should I pour wine?

CHENG TEH:

Sits down again.
I want you, my dear Big Sister, to pour wine into my cup with your own beautiful hands, and with your beautiful hands put the cup in my hand. Then guide the cup of wine to my lips. After I finish this cup of wine, I'll leave.
Waving his left sleeve.

LI FENG:

Is there sugar on my hands?

CHENG TEH:

No, there isn't . .

LI FENG:

Is there honey on my hands?

CHENG TEH:

No, there isn't any honey on your hands, either.

LI FENG:

Since there isn't any sugar nor any honey, why do you want me to pour wine for you?

Turns away from him and puts her hands on her hips.

CHENG TEH:

Men who are spendthrifts desire to have such comforts.

LI FENG:

Such comforts I hate to give.

CHENG TEH:

Are you going to pour or not?

LI FENG:

Takes a step away toward the right and puts her right hand on her hip.

I still refuse to pour.

CHENG TEH:

All right. You'd better return the piece of silver to me.

LI FENG:

Going downstage center, accompanied by the little drum.

I'll get it for you.

CHENG TEH:

Wait a moment. Do you know where I got the money?

LI FENG:

Turns around toward Cheng Teh.

You probably robbed a house!

CHENG TEH:

Exactly.

I big gong.

I broke into the royal house.

1 big gong.

If I'm not arrested, everything will be all right.

1 big gong.

But if I am arrested, then you and your brother will be involved in the crime.

2 big gongs.

I don't want the piece of silver now. I'm going.

Stands up and starts to go, accompanied by the little drum.

LI FENG:

Following him.

Sir, please come back and talk it over with me.

CHENG TEH:

There isn't anything to talk over.

LI FENG:

Talk it over!

2 beats on the little drum.

She puts the back of her right hand on her left cheek.

Talk it over!

2 beats on the little drum..

She puts the back of her left hand on her right cheek as she lowers her head.

CHENG TEH:

With whom do you want to talk it over?

LI FENG:

My heart wants to talk it over with my mouth.

CHENG TEH:

Goes back and sits down.

Hurry up and talk it over, then.

LI FENG:

Goes downstage right, accompanied by little drum.

Aside.

Ai-ya! Let me see!

Makes a circular movement with the third finger toward her right temple, accompanied by the little drum and the little gong.

His silver was stolen from the imperial palace. If he is not arrested, everything will be all right. But if he is arrested, my brother and I will be arrested too. What am I going to do?

3 beats on the little drum.

Oh, my brother,

Weeps, with her handkerchief over her eyes she shakes her head.

My dear brother!

2 beats on little drum.

Is this the way we'll end our business of selling wine?

Goes back to Cheng Teh, *accompanied by the little drum.*

As she pours wine.

I, Li Feng, pour out a cup of wine and ask the Lord Soldier to accept graciously and drink it.

CHENG TEH:

I am going to tease her to see if she has any feelings.

To Li Feng *and puts his fan on the back of her hand.*

Dry cup!

He holds up his left sleeve in front of his face, downs the wine and tickles Li Feng's *palm.*

4 beats on little drum and little gong.

LI FENG:

Jumps up, turns away, stamps her foot.

Dry cup to your mother![2]

CHENG TEH:

Why do you curse me?

LI FENG:

If you want to drink, go on and drink. Why did you have to scratch my palm? What for?

---

2. Reference to one's mother in this way is a Chinese vulgarity, an allusion to a strong curse.

CHENG TEH:

Oh, since I haven't been hunting with my bow and arrows these days, my nails have grown. I must have accidentally touched you a little with my fingernails.

LI FENG:

My nails are long, too; but they aren't touching you.

Points at him.

CHENG TEH:

Stands up and walks up to her.

I can see Big Sister likes to take advantage of others. Come here, come here and tickle my rough hands if you like, Big Sister.

He stretches out his palm for her to tickle.

LI FENG:

Sir, if you ask for it . . .

CHENG TEH:

Come on and tickle me.

LI FENG:

Takes a step to the right.

No, I won't.

CHENG TEH:

Why not?

He runs away to the left.

LI FENG:

Look at you! I haven't started tickling and yet you are running away already.

CHENG TEH:

Comes back to her.

I promise I won't run away.

LI FENG:

If so, I'll tickle

Drum, gong.

Tickle

Drum, gong.

Tickle!

Drum, gong, gong.

She tickles Cheng Teh's *hand.*

CHENG TEH:

Laughs.

Ha, ha, ha!

LI FENG:

Singing hsi-p'i-liu-shiu-pan from the tape recorded from the original.

The silvery new moon
Is shining over the earth.
Where do you come from,
My good sir?

CHENG TEH:

Big Sister, don't ask me questions.
I live on earth and beneath the sky.

LI FENG:

Speaks

You fool! Everybody lives on earth and beneath the sky. Do you suppose anyone can live above the sky?

CHENG TEH:

Ah, Big Sister, my lodging is different from anybody else's.

LI FENG:

How differnet?

CHENG TEH:

Far, farway in the city of Peking,

Waves his long sleeve to the left.

There is a large circle,

Makes a large circle with his folded fan, little gong and cymbals.

Within which there is a small circle,

Little gong and cymbals as he makes a smaller circle with his fan.

Within which there is a yellow circle,

Making a still smaller circle with his fan followed by little gong.

And it is within that yellow circle where I live,

A little gong as he points with his fan.

LI FENG:

Now I know who you are.

CHENG TEH:

Who am I?

LI FENG:

You are my brother . . .

CHENG TEH:

Ay!

LI FENG:

. . . . My brother's brother-in-law[3].

CHENG TEH:

Huh! What nonsense!

He shakes his right sleeve and turns away to the left.

LI FENG:

Mr. Soldier's manners are really too outrageous.
You shouldn't try seduction of a decent girl.

CHENG TEH:

Decent girl! Oh, what a decent girl!

---

3. Reference to any member of a family in this manner was considered to be very rude.

You shouldn't wear a cherry-apple blossom in your hair,
Or smile and giggle to attract a person's love,
But it all comes down to this cherry-apple blossom
Points with his fan at the flower in her hair.

LI FENG:

Cherry-apple blossom!
Oh, what a cherry-apple blossom!
Takes the flower and looks at it.
How it makes you tease me so!
Let me throw it on the floor.
She throws the flower on the floor.
3 beats on drum.
Throw it and stamp on it.
Little gong, little gong.
From now on, I'll never wear this cherry-apple flower!
Big gong.

CHENG TEH:

Li Feng's manners are really too outrageous,
To destroy this cherry-apple flower!
Let me pick it up for you.
He picks it up.
Let me put –put–put–put.
Drum.
put
Drum.
put
Drum, Drum.
On you this cherry-apple, flower!
He puts the flower in her hair.

LI FENG:

I am so upset and frightened.
I'd better run away and escape into my bedroom.
Li Feng *runs away, crosses the "threshold" and exits to left, back of stage, accompanied by little drum.*

CHENG TEH:

Crosses the "threshold".

Let her go,
Let her run,
May it be as far as to the sea or the ocean,
I can always catch her,
Follow her even to the end of the earth!

Exit Cheng Teh *to the left, accompanied by the little gong.*

The Property Man *appears from upstage left, puts the chair in front of the table with soft playing of the cymbals and the gong*

SCENE TWO

The setting is the same, Center stage, however, is now Li Feng's *bedroom.* *Enter* Li Feng *from the right, accompanied by the little drum.*

LI FENG:

Comes to downstage center.

Here comes Li Feng.

Enter Cheng Teh *from the right.*

CHENG TEH:

With Cheng Teh following close by!

LI FENG:

Steps over imaginary threshold into her bedroom, center downstage, and gestures to close and fasten the door.

I must shut the door.

She carries the chair to downstage center, with its back toward the audience, accompanied by little drum and gong.

CHENG TEH:

Gestures to knock on the door with his fan, accompanied by 2 beats of the wooden clapper at a time.

Big Sister, open the door, quick!

Knocks again.

Open the door, Big Sister.

Knocks again.

The invisible door is between them and Li Feng *stands facing the audience and with her hand on the back of the chair.*

LI FENG:

No, I won't.

CHENG TEH:

Why not?

LI FENG:

Not until my brother comes back.

CHENG TEH:

Your brother won't come home tonight.

LI FENG:

Then I will not open it tonight.

CHENG TEH:

He won't come home in ten days.

LI FENG:

Then I will not open it in ten days.

CHENG TEH:

He will never come home.

LI FENG:

Then I will never open it!

CHENG TEH:

Walks to downstage right and strokes his beard. Aside.

Hm-m, let me see, This lass won't open the door until her brother comes back. What shall I do?

3 drum beats i clapper.

I've got it.

Little gong

Let me play a trick on her.

Aloud and toward Li Feng.

Oh, Mr. Li Lung! So you're back at last. The food is cold, the wine is bad in your hotel, and there is no service whatsoever. Please give me the check and I'll leave here at once!

LI FENG:

Oh, My brother is back! Let me open the door.

She carries the chair back and places it in front of the table, accompanied by the little drum. She goes to downstage center and gestures to pull the bolt and open the door, steps over the imaginary threshold and goes to the left, looking for his brother.

Where is my brother?

All this while Cheng Teh has his back toward her and as soon as she comes out, Cheng Teh *quickly slips into the room by crossing over the imaginary threshold. When she returns to her room, she is surprised and furious to find* Cheng Teh *sitting with his fan in front of his face there. The movements are accompanied by drum and the little gong.*

Where is my brother? . . . .

CHENG TEH:

Big gong.

Here.

Lowering his fan.

LI FENG:

T'sui, you rascal! You followed me from the front room to the backyard, and from the backyard to my bedroom. Why?

Little gong.

CHENG TEH:

I want you to give me something to send me off with.

LI FENG:

Oh, so you are a beggar! Just a minute. I'll get you a penny to send you off.

Prepares to go.

CEHGN TEH:

A big girl like you should know what to send me off with.

LI FENG:

Goes around the table and to stage center.

I understand, but I'm frightened.

Little drum and little gong.

CHENG TEH:

Frightened of what?

LI FENG:

Of my brother coming back.

CHENG TEH:

Oh, I'll be here if he comes back.

LI FENG:

Exactly! If you're here, then I'm not! So you'd better leave, quickly!

Little gong.

CHENG TEH:

Puts his hands behind on his back.

I refuse to go.

Big gong.

LI FENG:

If you don't, I'll scream!

Little gong.

CHENG TEH:

Scream what?

LI FENG:

Scream that you're killing people!

CHENG TEH:

Without any weapons, how can I murder anyone?

LI FENG:

Points at him.

Your heart is sharper than a knife!

CHENG TEH:

Stands firm with hands on back.

I just won't get out.

LI FENG:

Comes downstage.

Then I'll scream. Ah . . . .

Little gong, little gong, cymbal.

CHENG TEH:

Wait! Just a moment.

LI FENG:

Waves her handkerchief at him.

Big gong.

Then get out at once!

CHENG TEH:

Goes to downstage right.

Aside.

Now, if this girl should really scream, she will wake up all the people in this town. That will be quite inconvenient.

1 drum beat.

Ah, well!

2 drum beats.

If she has good fortune, she is going to be a lady in my *court;* if not, I will leave here at once.

Big gong.

Goes to the chair and sits down again.

Big Sister, do you recognize me?

LI FENG:

You are a little brother of a number-one house (*puts up her right thumb, accompanied by the little gong)* and the big brother of a number-three house.

Puts up her index and third fingers in her left hand.

You are a number-two ass!

2 drum beats and 1 big gong as she points at Cheng Teh.

CHENG TEH:

Ay! Stop cursing. I am no other than the Emperor, Cheng Teh!

2 big gong beats and cymbals.

LI FENG:

Go on! *(Shoves* Cheng Teh *from the chair and sits down herself.)* Do you know who I am?

She puts her hands on her hips.

CHENG TEH:

Of course, I do. You are a wine girl in the town of the Plum Dragon.

LI FENG:

Huh! I am no other than the mother of the present Emperor, Cheng Teh.

Gong, cymbal, big gong.

CHENG TEH:

What an imprudent and outrageous remark, you country lass! Ever since the beginning of time, an emperor has always worn precious things.

LI FENG:

Then show your precious things.

CHENG TEH:

If I don't have any . . .

LI FENG:

Then show your mother's.

CHENG TEH:

Don't curse, Big Sister, but look!

Li Feng gets up and looks.

The Property Man *enters from right back of stage and helps* Cheng Teh *take off the hood.*

Taking off my hood and opening my gown to show my dragon[4] robe, I ask Big Sister to look. There are dragons on my head, dragons on my gown, dragons left and right, front and back. There are altogether nine dragons on my robe–golden dragons with five claws too. Now who am I, Big Sister?

Cheng Teh *puts his right foot on the chair to show* Li Feng *his dragon robe.*

LI FENG:

Amazed.

Ah, what precious things! *She tries to feel his robe but Cheng Teh gestures that boy and girl should not touch each other. Then he sits down.* No wonder last night I had a dream about a golden dragon with five claws descending on this room.

Singing "erh-huang-ping-pan" from the tape.

Allow me to come forward and kneel so this slave can be pardoned and be ennobled.

Cheng Teh *sits down on the chair in front of the table.* The Property Man *puts a red cushion on the floor in front of* Cheng Teh *for* Li Feng *to kneel.*

Long live the Emperor!

Little drum and big gong.

Li Feng *kneels before* Cheng Teh *with her back toward the audience.*

CHENG TEH:

Who is this that is kneeling before me?

LI FENG:

Li Feng, Your Majesty.

Little gong.

CHENG TEH:

Waving his sleeve.

---

4. The dragon–the imperial emblem.

What is your wish?

Big gong.

LI FENG:

That I be granted the title of a lady in your court,
Your Majesty.

Little gong.

CHENG TEH:

Just now you offended me by saying I was your brother's big brother-in-law, so I am not going to ennoble you.

Big gong.

LI FENG:

If you make me a lady, then my brother will be your big brother-in-law.

Little gong.

CHENG TEH:

Not even to become a younger brother-in-law!

Big gong.

LI FENG:

Oh, Your Majesty, please do make me a lady, even if it's in the lowest rank.

CHENG TEH:

No, I won't.

Big gong.

LI FENG:

Just a tiny bit of a lady, please.

Cymbal.

CHENG TEH:

No.

Big gong.

LI FENG:

Just a wee-wee bit of a lady, please.

Cymbal.

CHENG TEH:

No, not even that.

Big gong.

LI FENG:

All right, if that's the case . . . .

Gets up and starts to go, accompanied by little drum and little gong.

CHENG TEH:

Wait.

Big gong.

If I don't grant you the title of a lady, what a disgrace it will be to you, my dear girl!

LI FENG:

It's all your fault.

CHENG TEH:

My three palaces and six courts are all full, but I can squeeze you in somewhere! All right, come, come, I'll ennoble you. I, Emperor Cheng Teh, hereby proclaim you a lady of the Sixth Court of the Third Palace!

Big gong, Big gong.

LI FENG:

Kneeling before Cheng Teh.

I kneel and knowtow to show my respect and gratitude.

CHENG TEH:

Stands up and helps Li Feng *up.*

With my royal hands, I help my darling lady up from the floor.

LI FENG:

Rises.

May I ask where Your Majesty wishes to go?

CHENG TEH:

Take me to my horse and let us leave for the palace.

Big gong.

LI FENG:

Your Majesty has certainly honored our humble town of the Plum tonight.

Little gong.

CHENG TEH AND LI FENG:

Together.

A real dragon has descended on a pair of golden cups.

Little gong, cymbal, big gong.

LI FENG:

Your Majesty, this way, please.

Pointing to the left.

CHENG TEH:

Where to?

LI FENG:

To my bedroom.

CHENG TEH:

Ai-ya-ya. I'm frightened!

3 drum beats.

LI FENG:

Of what?

CHENG TEH:

Of your brother who'll come back soon.

LI FENG:

But now you have me, an empress, to protect you.

CHENG TEH:

That's right. As long as I have you, I have nothing to fear. So let's go, my dear Li Feng.

Little gong.

LI FENG:

Curtsies with hands folded on the left side.

Your Majesty!

Big gong.

CHENG TEH:

My Empress!

Big gong.

LI FENG:

Long live the Emperor.

Big gong, big gong.

CHENG TEH:

Laughing.

Now to *our* palace!

Li Feng *goes first.*

Cheng Teh *and* Li Feng *both go off to upstage left.*

Chinese music from tape.

ABOUT THE WRITER

Realizing that drama is the best means to promote international understanding, Josephine Huang Hung has written many articles and books in English on Chinese drama in the attempt to introduce it to the West. As a visiting professor under the Fulbright-Hays Act, she herself produced *The Price of Wine* at Grinnell College, Iowa, in 1963, and *One Missing Head* at the University of North Carolina at Greensboro, in 1967.

Born in Tientsin, North China, and a graduate of Yenching University, Peiping, she received her M.A. from Columbia University. After her return to China, she became a professor in various universities in Chungking and Shanghai. Since 1948, she has been a professor of western drama at National Taiwan University. She is a member of the American Educational Theatre Association, Association of Asian Studies and the P.E.N. Club. She is also a judge for the Dramatic Productions for Appreciation for the promotion of the Little Theatre Movement in Free China. She is teaching Chinese drama as a visiting professor at Michigan State University in the academic year of 1970-1971.

Her publications in English include a textbook, *A Treasury of Western Drama,* published in 1958 (second edition, 1961); "The Tea-Picker Girl," a one-act play, (*China Today,* January 1959); "The Chinese Opera as an Art," (*China Today,* March 1958); "The Chinese Drama," (translated from Dr. Chi Ju-shan's "Chinese Drama"; *China Today.* April 1959). "Chinese Drama, Yesterday and Today "(*Free China Review,* vol.2, No.12, Dec. 1961); "The Unique Art of Chinese Opera," (*Journal of the China Society,* vol.5, 1965 and *Ming Drama,* Heritage press, 1966.) She is one of the co-authors of *Fernstliches Theater,* edited by Heins Kindermann, published by Alfred Kroner Verlag, Stuttgart, Germany, 1966. In Chinese her publications include: "The Personality of Shakespeare," (*New Tide,* April 1958); and "Sophocles and His Tragic Art," (*Literary Review,* January 1960).

BIBLIOGRAPHY The Western Language

Arlington, L. C. *The Chinese Drama from the Earliest Times Until Today.* Shanghai: Kelly and Walsh, 1930, reissued by Benjamin Blom, Inc. N.Y. 1966

Arlington, L. C., and Acton, Harold. *Famous Plays Chinese.* Peiping: Henri Vetch, 1937, reprinted by Russell, U.S.A. 1967.

Buss, Kate. *Studies in the Chinese Drama.* New York: Jonathan Cape and H. Smith, 1930.

Chen, Jack. *The Chinese Theatre.* London: Dennis Dobson, Ltd., 1949.

Eberhard, Wolfram. *A History of China* (translated by E. W. Dickes). Berkeley: University of California Press, 1950.

Giles, Herbert A. *A History of Chinese Literature.* New York: D. Appleton and Company, 1931 (revised edition).

Giles, Herbert Allen: *Gems of Chinese Literature,* Paragon, N.Y. 1967.

Hart, Henry H. *The West Chamber, A Medieval Drama.* Stanford: Standford University Press, 1936.

Hung, Vosephine Huang: *Das Chinesische Theater,* in *Fernstliches Theater,* edited by Heinz Kindermann, Alfred Kroner Verlag, Stuttgart, Germany, 1966.

Kao, George, *Chinese Wit and Humor.* New York: Coward-McCann, 1946.

Lewis, John H.: *Foundations of Chinese Musical Art,* Paragon, N.Y. 1967.

Sachs, Court, *The Rise of Music in the Ancient World, East and West.* New York: W. W. Norton and Company. 1943.

Scott, A. C. *The Classical Theatre of China.* London: George Allen and Unwin, 1957.

Scott, A. C. *An Introduction to the Chinese Theatre.* Singapore: Donald Moore, 1958.

Scott, A. C.: *Traditional Chinese Plays:* "The Butterfly Dream" and "Ssu Lang Visits His Mother" The University of Wisconsin Press, Madison, Milwaukee and London, 1967.

Tsiang Un-kai. *K'ouen K'iu, Le Theatre Chinois Ancien.* Paris: Librarie Ernest Leroux, 1932.

Yang, Daniel Shih-p'êng: An Annotated Bibliography of Materials for the Study *of the Peking Theatre*, *Wisconsin China Series, No. 2,* The University of Wisconsin, 1967.

Zucker, A. E. *The Chinese Theatre.* Boston: Little, Brown and Company, 1925.

Zung, Cecilia S. C. *Secrets of the Chinese Drama.* Shanghai: Kelly and Walsh, 1937, reprinted by Benjamin Blom Inc. N. Y. 1964.

BIBLIOGRAPHY **The Chinese Language**

Chiang Tso-tung 姜作棟 Lin Po-nien 林柏年, and Lin Hsiao-han 李效厂 (editors). *Hsiu-ting P'ing-chü Hsuan* 修訂平劇選 . Taipei: Chung Cheng Book Co., 1958.

Ch'i Ju-shan 齊如山 . *Ching-Chü chih Pien-ch'ien* 京劇之變遷 Peiping: 1935.

Ch'i Ju-shan 齊如山. *Kuo-chü Kai-lun* 國劇概論 . Taipei: Wen-yi Ch'uang-tso She, 1953.

Ch'i Ju-shan 齊如山. *Kuo-chü Man-t'an* 國劇漫談 . Taipei: 1954.

Ch'i Ju-shan: 齊如山 , *Ch'i Ju-shan Ch'üan-chi* 齊如山全集・九冊 *(The Complete Works of Ch'i Ju-shan),* Taipei; Ch'i Ju-shan hsien sheng i-chu pien yin wei-yüan-hui, 1964 (9 volumes)

Hsu Mu-yun 徐慕雲. *Li-Yüan Ying Shih* 梨園影事 . Shanghai: China Printing Co., 1933.

Kao I-san 高宜三 : *Kuo-chü-yuan* 國劇藝苑 *The Artistic Content of the Peking Opera*, Taiwan: Yang-kuang Ch'u pan shê 1964.

Meng Yao, 孟瑤 : Chung Kuo Hsi Ch'ü Shih 中國戲劇史 *(A History of Chinese Drama)* 4 Vols. Taipei: Wen Hsing Collectanea, No. 150, Taiwan World Book Company. 1965.

Shih Ling 石玲 (editor). *P'ing-chü Kao* 平劇考 (3 vols.). Taipei: Ch'i Yüan Publishing Co., 1956.

Ti Yi Wen-hua She 第一文化社 (editors). *Kuo-chü Chi-ch'eng* 國劇集成 (8 vols.). Taipei: Ti Yi Wen-hua She, 1956.